Quiet
Moments
for ministry wives

Quiet Moments

for ministry wives

SCRIPTURES,

MEDITATIONS,

& PRAYERS

compiled by joyce williams

BEACON HILL PRESS
OF KANSAS CITY

Printed in the
United States of America

Cover Design: Darlene Filley
Cover Photo: Jupiter Images
Interior Design: Sharon Page

All Scripture quotations not otherwise designated are from the *Holy Bible, New International Version*® (NIV®). Copyright © 1973, 1978, 1984 by International Bible Society. Used by permission of Zondervan Publishing House. All rights reserved.

Permission to quote from the following additional copyrighted versions of the Bible is acknowledged with appreciation:

The *New American Standard Bible*® (NASB®), © copyright The Lockman Foundation 1960, 1962, 1963, 1968, 1971, 1972, 1973, 1975, 1977, 1995.

The *New King James Version* (NKJV). Copyright © 1979, 1980, 1982 Thomas Nelson, Inc.

The *Holy Bible, New Living Translation* (NLT), copyright © 1996. Used by permission of Tyndale House Publishers, Inc., Wheaton, IL 60189. All rights reserved.

Today's English Version (TEV). Copyright by American Bible Society, 1966, 1971, 1976, 1992.

The *Living Bible* (TLB), © 1971. Used by permission of Tyndale House Publishers, Inc., Wheaton, IL 60189. All rights reserved.

The *Message* (TM). Copyright © 1993, 1994, 1995, 1996, 2000, 2001, 2002. Used by permission of NavPress Publishing Group.

Scripture quotations marked KJV are from the King James Version.

Library of Congress Cataloging-in-Publication Data

Quiet moments for ministry wives : scriptures, meditations, and prayers / compiled by Joyce Williams.
    p. cm.
    ISBN 0-8341-2261-8 (pbk.)
    1. Spouses of clergy—Prayer-books and devotions—English. 2. Wives—Prayer-books and devotions—English. I. Williams, Joyce, 1944-

    BV4395.Q85 2006
    242'.69—dc22

                  2006007998

10 9 8 7 6 5 4 3 2 1

CONTENTS

Foreword, by Norma Smalley   7

Preface, by Cynthia Heald   9

Acknowledgments   11

Introduction, by Jeannie McCullough   13

1. Gladys Staines: A God Worth Dying For   15
2. Joyce Williams: Be Still and Know   23
3. Joyce Baggott: Wait—Don't Worry   27
4. Sheila Bird: A Safe Place   30
5. Cindy Blasdel: A Forgiven Forgiver   33
6. Sally Bond: Wings for Ministry   36
7. Vonette Bright: Fruits of Our Labors   39
8. Jennifer Buettner: The God Who Will Not Forget You   42
9. Myrna Buhler: I Don't Know Who I Am   46
10. Joyce Williams: Lambs into the Fold   49
11. Rachael Crabb: Moving into the Neighborhood   52
12. Betty Daily: Bible School at the City Dump   55
13. Susan Dillow: Release and Wait   58
14. Denise Franklin: Beauty in the Journey   61
15. Kendra Graham: My First Love   64
16. Joyce Williams: A Cup of Cold Lemonade   67
17. Karan Gunter: Fix Your Eyes   71
18. Patty Hambrick: Called by Marriage? Called by God?   74
19. Debbie Henry: Made for Ministry   78
20. Mary Alice Hoover: How Much Can You Afford?   81
21. Joyce Williams: Riding Through the Rainbows   84
22. Joyce Jothi: God's Faithfulness   88

23. Debbie Keener: Pain Passes. Beauty Remains — 91

24. Linda Lewis: Crisis Peace — 94

25. Gail MacDonald: Coming to Him — 97

26. Edie MacPherson: A Step of Faith — 101

27. Ellen McWhirter: Our Faithful Guide — 104

28. Joyce Mehl: When Love Is Not Enough — 108

29. Annie Montgomery: A Very Present Help — 112

30. Joyce Williams: Robins Don't Have Wrinkles — 115

31. Pam Morgan: Guard Your Heart — 118

32. Kelly Pankratz: Too Broken to Trust — 121

33. Jodie Pinckard: Life Is Still Happening — 124

34. Nancy Roberts: Chocolates and Trials — 128

35. Cheryl Roland: Trust, Adjust, and Obey — 131

36. Pam Runyan: For You I Wait All Day Long — 134

37. Gayla Ryan: Victim or Victor — 137

38. Joyce Williams: Angel and Blessing from the Jungle — 141

39. Cindy Schmelzenbach: Ordinary or Sacred? — 144

40. Laisa Siakimotu: Perfect Peace — 147

41. Joyce Williams: The Day We Crossed Kellogg — 151

42. Frances Simpson: God's Formula — 158

43. Mary Tabb: Hurricanes, Eagles, and Baby Prayers — 161

44. Joyce Williams: Loving Her Neighbor — 166

45. Melody Tunney: God Is Speaking. Are You Listening? — 169

46. Sharon Joy Underwood: Unexpected Waves, Unexpected Blessings — 173

47. Joyce Williams: Partnering with Angel — 177

48. Joyce Williams: Quiet Moments — 181

About the Contributors — 183

FOREWORD
norma smalley

Quiet Moments for Ministry Wives? I must confess—this title appeared to me to be somewhat of an oxymoron. My husband, Gary, and I are privileged to work with many pastors around the world whose flocks demand enormous attention. So finding time to "be still" can be quite a challenge for ministers and their spouses.

This book is a challenge to all of us who are on the frontlines of ministry to make withdrawing to solitary places to commune with our Lord a priority. That's when we experience the renewal and restoration we must have. Then, as we reenter our mission fields, we are refreshed for the day ahead.

As a ministry wife, I have found that it makes such a difference when I start my day remembering that trials and irritations will come every day. Our Father promises in Rom. 8:28 to take each one and turn it into good. So when trials come, I make myself say, *Today is my gift. Lord, you are good, and I trust you!*

I encourage you to embrace each brand-new day as your gift. Then take a few moments to come apart and read these meditations so that your heart will be warmed and your soul refreshed.

PREFACE
cynthia heald

"Be still, and know that I am God" (Ps. 46:10) is one of my favorite Bible verses. I've always been touched that God would so graciously invite us to sit in His presence in order to deepen our intimacy with Him.

I thought this was such a tender call to closeness until I took time to study the true meaning of "be still." What I discovered was that the Lord was not offering a respite to the harassed but was in essence trying to get our attention in the midst of our busy lives so that our focus was on His sufficiency and not on our circumstances.

I realized that His "Be silent" or "Cease striving" was reminiscent of my taking my small, restless children by the shoulders, looking them in the eyes, and sternly saying, "Be still!"

But it's His abiding love that compels His call to stillness and to a more profound understanding of who He is. For as we journey through difficult valleys and climb seemingly insurmountable mountains, He of necessity sternly bids us to turn away from the hardships and the daily routines of our lives so that we can experience the comfort only His presence can bring.

The truth of this scripture and the consolation it brings is found in the testimonies of the dear women in this book. Joyce Williams and other choice servants of the Lord share their stories of learning to be still. These are women who are in the "trenches"—serving alongside their husbands, learning through adversity and the stress of being in ministry how essential it is to listen to God, to stop, and to be quiet before Him.

I pray that you'll be challenged and encouraged, as I have been, to realize that our being still is a gift He gives to us—a priceless gift of knowing Him in silence and gaining strength in quietness.

"In quietness and confidence is your strength" (Isa. 30:15, NLT).

ACKNOWLEDGMENTS

I thank God for His inspiration and guidance in enabling me to work on this project. It has been awesome to watch as He directed my path to just the right contributors—one right after the other. Each devotional in this book has a unique "story behind the story." I wish I could share each one with you!

First of all, I must express a special word of appreciation to each ministry wife who took time out of her very busy schedule to participate in this project.

And again, I must thank my dear husband, Gene, for his ongoing encouragement and faith in me. None of my books would have been written without his enthusiastic support and editing.

Bonnie, Judi, and the rest of the wonderful staff at Beacon Hill Press of Kansas City have once again been the best. Thanks so much for believing in this devotional book.

As always, my prayer is that you, the reader, will find encouragement and renewal as you soak up these pages. May you enjoy precious quiet moments with our Heavenly Father that will tickle your heart and restore your soul.

INTRODUCTION
jeannie mccullough

*Do not store up for yourselves treasures on earth, where moth
and rust destroy, and where thieves break in and steal. But
store up for yourselves treasures in heaven, where moth and rust
do not destroy, and where thieves do not break in and steal.
For where your treasure is, there your heart will be also.*
—Matt. 6:19-21

Who knows what we were thinking, but when I was sweet
16, Mel asked my father if he could marry me. Three hours
later he promised my dad to protect, provide—and postpone
the event until he had struck gold or something like that. You
know, the "impossible."

When we were married three years later, Mel had not
struck gold. My wedding ring cost $23.00. Thirty-five years
later, Mel gave me a diamond. But my life even before I
received that diamond was full of precious jewels that God
gave me—Mel being the first one.

Some of my finest jewels have been the people I have
known—especially the ones God sent to serve alongside me
in ministry. Over the years their encouragement has come to
me in many ways—hugs, smiles, understanding, gifts, accep-
tance, cards, and many letters.

Twenty-five years ago I started the practice of hiding away
these written "jewels." I have tucked notes in purses that were

pretty but rarely carried, in closets that were condemned because of clutter, and pantries that were piled high with towels used only in panic. Then I depended on God to lead me to my hidden jewels when my soul was sagging. These discoveries have made the old seem new again.

Recently I ran across a "diamond" in my nightstand drawer. First I looked to see who had written it. It was indeed one of those 10-karat jewels from a friend—a follower of Christ and a faithful servant who now has been sidelined by the infirmities of body and mind. Yet her arms of love are still holding me with the note she wrote to me long ago reminding me that she was just one of my many friends who love me. Even though the letter was folded a little askew and her handwriting was at a slight angle, tucked away in these imperfections was a godly aroma—you know, the kind that arouses the soul.

As the written jewels I have hidden away in my home have encouraged me over the years, my prayer is that this collection of written jewels from ministry wives will encourage you.

1

A GOD WORTH DYING FOR

gladys staines

For to me, to live is Christ and to die is gain.
—Phil. 1:21

Tears rolled down my cheeks early on the morning of January 14, 1999, during my quiet time with the Lord. I had been reading the story of Abraham's obedience, but what touched me most was the story in my devotional of a 12-year-old girl who was going blind. She told her pastor when he visited her that God was taking her sight. The wise pastor said, "Don't let Him." She questioned this. Then he said, "Offer your sight as a sacrifice to Him." That was when the question was posed to me.

As I prayed and listened, I felt an inner voice asking me whether I was willing to give all I love—maybe even my husband, children, and possessions—for Him. I recall that I spent a lot of time on this question. Then I told Him, *Lord Jesus, yes, I am willing. Take all I have for your use—my husband, children, and everything else I have. I surrender them all to you.* The Lord comforted me by saying, *Don't you know that Abraham pleased me by sacrificing his only son, Isaac?*

I had no way of knowing that only nine days later my husband, Graham, along with our two sons, Philip and Timothy, would be ambushed in Manoharpur. As they huddled together in our station wagon they were burned alive by a frenzied mob with flaming torches. Oh, how I thank God for the way He had prepared my heart to be willing to surrender all that I love! Our faith in God sustained our daughter, Esther, and me during the horrible reality of our loss.

At first I was told that only the station wagon had been damaged. Later word came that there had been an "incident" at the camp and that Graham and the boys were missing. Finally a government official broke the news that they were dead. After my initial shock, I found Esther. I tenderly put my arms around her and whispered, "We've been left alone."

The nightmare atmosphere of the next few days, weeks, and months was cushioned by the knowledge that God had prepared my heart to surrender my loved ones. Even as we learned the details of the gruesome murders, Esther and I clung to each other and to our faith in God. I felt the peace that passes understanding sweep over me as I reflected on our lives together. As I shared those memories with Esther, she, too, found great comfort.

Although at one point we had lived only 70 kilometers apart in Australia, Graham and I had never seen each other until we met in 1981 in India, where I had gone with a mission training organization. Graham was already serving there as a missionary. We were married in August 1983. Graham returned to India after seven months, and I joined him at the

Mayurbhanj Leprosy Home near Baripada, Orissa. He had served Christ and leprosy sufferers there since 1965, and it quickly became our shared labor of love.

Graham was a great missionary, husband, and father. In spite of his very hectic lifestyle, he always had time for the children and me. He was kind and gentle and did all things for the glory of the Lord. He never worried, even when facing dire needs. He always praised God and never appealed to people for help, because as a child of the King of Kings he said, "Why should I appeal to human beings for help?" We were one in faith, vision, and mission.

We lived in an old bungalow within the mission compound and chose a very simple lifestyle. We counted our three children, Esther, Philip, and Timothy, as gifts from God to be nurtured in godly ways. Although we missed them terribly when we eventually had to send Esther and Philip 2,000 kilometers away for schooling, Graham and I were happy about their spiritual environment.

Both Esther and Philip loved the leprosy ministry when they were home from school. Philip dressed his friends' wounds like an experienced medical person. Tim loved to "preach." He often set up chairs in the lounge, placed local language books on them, and pretended they were the congregation. All three of our children loved the Lord, the people, and singing. Timothy especially enjoyed making up his own songs and singing them.

In 1996 our family visited Australia. Somehow it no longer felt like home. All of us were glad to get back to the only home we knew with our "family" in Mayurbhanj. We counted

it as a great blessing to serve in such a wonderful mission helping many to live with dignity.

On that night, January 22, 1999, it's likely that Graham reflected on the wonderful life we had shared serving the Lord
together. He and our boys always enjoyed the camping trips
to Manoharpur. He had parked the station wagon near the
church. They had shared dinner with friends and then went
out to the station wagon. As Graham tucked in Philip and Timothy and prayed with them, I believe his heart was filled with
joy. I picture him praising God as he drew a straw pad over
the roof of the station wagon to shelter the boys from the
cold winds. Then he lay down with them. Eyewitnesses have
shared what they saw and heard.

About midnight drums began beating approximately 100
meters away as a group of young Santhals swayed in a traditional Dangri dance. They joined another group led by Dara
Singh, a troublemaker whose name was a familiar one in police
records throughout the area. They worked themselves into
an enraged frenzy. The shouting, screaming mob of 50 or 60
with burning torches in their hands then converged on the
campsite where Graham and our boys were sleeping. They
were shouting as they ripped off the straw pad that covered
the vehicle. Then they started smashing the windows of the
station wagon with bars and sticks. The frenzied crowd
blocked Graham from escaping with our sons. They thrust
open the doors of the station wagon, and later reports sus-
pected that they brutally beat and stabbed all three of them
with tridents, which are sharp, three-pronged, forklike weap-

ons. As Graham and our two little boys lay huddled together in a final embrace, someone placed a bundle of straw inside the station wagon, and the mob lit a fire. My precious husband and sons were incinerated as the flames consumed them. The killers stood there and watched the three of them roast alive as the fire burned them and the vehicle.

The attackers had blocked the villagers' huts so they could not help my husband and sons. When Hansda, our station wagon driver and coworker, broke loose and tried to pour water onto the fire, he was savagely beaten and chased away. As he later recounted his horror and agony to me, between sobs he said, "My parents were cured leprosy sufferers and lived at the rehabilitation center. I was born there. You treated me like a son. Our children played together." As he continued to weep, his tears of sorrow splashed onto the ground while I tried to comfort him.

A number of villagers who were eyewitnesses said they saw a wide beam of bright light shining from above that came to rest on the burning station wagon. I believe that my husband and children were especially strengthened by my Lord and angels from heaven. After the frenzied mob left, Gilbert Venz, a friend of ours from Australia, was finally able to push aside the barriers blocking the door to his hut. He rushed to the vehicle only to find the burned-out shell and three bodies. He said that although they were charred beyond recognition, Graham and our sons were locked in an embrace. Even in death they had been inseparable. Gilbert said, "We couldn't believe what we saw. We were numbed. . . . Graham was an embodiment of Christian love and compassion. And your children—tender and cheerful—used to play with the leprosy sufferers and their children. Is there not a limit to man's wickedness?"

Many expressions of condolence came in from around the world. India's President K. R. Narayanan said these murders "belong in the inventory of mankind's blackest deeds." Editor Abhay Mokasi wrote, "Graham Staines converted leprosy patients into human beings, for the treatment meted out to them [lepers] even by their near and dear ones was worse than that given to animals. The Hindu fundamentalists responsible for killing Staines and his two sons should know that the loss of these three lives is not just to Christianity but to humanity at large. The Hindu leprosy patients, to whom he devoted his life, have lost their saviour."

I must confess that the loss of Graham and our sons has been a real test of our faith. Esther and I comforted each other as we walked through the valley of the shadow of death. When the flower-bedecked caskets arrived, thousands were waiting to pay tribute to "Shahibu." The residents at the leprosy home were beside themselves with grief, and I found that Esther and I were the only ones who could console them. We sat on the ground with them right by the three caskets. Many joined with us as we shared Bible verses and sang in Santhali the words from hymns.

I remember noticing the beautiful roses and saying, "Timothy loved roses. It was so nice of you to put so many roses here."

At the memorial service Esther said, "I praise the Lord that He found my father worthy to die for Him." She and I found great comfort in singing together "Because He Lives." And we have truly found the wonderful words of that song to be true.

We wanted to reassure the people of India. I told them that I had just one message. "I'm not bitter. Neither am I angry. I can forgive their killers' deeds. I have forgiven them. Only Jesus can forgive their sins. But they will have to ask. I have one great desire: that each citizen of this country should establish a personal relationship with Jesus Christ, who gave His life for his or her sins. Every person should know that Jesus loves him or her, and in turn each one should trust Him and endeavor to love others. Let us burn hatred and spread the flame of Christ's love."

Many people asked me if I was afraid of the rabid groups and if I had plans to leave India. My answer was "Why should I be afraid? Here people support and love us. I cannot leave. After all, the leprosy sufferers need to be taken care of."

Although I received another blow in May 1999 when my mother passed away in Australia, I can still say that in spite of all the trials, my faith in my Lord remains unshakable. I really missed Esther when she returned to continue her studies at Hebron School many kilometers away, but the Lord helped me.

Since my husband had always done the work of five people, and I was basically a housewife, I was really challenged. But by God's grace I followed His plan and remained in Baripada to continue the work. My prayer continuously is *Lord, I can't do it alone.* But I gladly agree with the words on Graham's framed poster in our home: "The Lord is my rock, my fortress." And I know I am never alone.

Gladys Staines remained in Baripade until 2004, planning and raising funds for the Graham Staines Memorial Hospital, which has now been completed. She and Esther returned that year to Australia, where Gladys cares for her 91-year-old father and Esther is a university student.

The World Evangelical Fellowship estimates that more than 150 million Christians have lost their lives for the faith during the 20th century and that it will be known as "the century of martyrs."

When Gladys left India, she challenged those she left behind:

Be faithful to whatever you are called to do. Never yield to the temptation to go back; never say "quit," even if there is persecution or threat. And like Graham and our sons, I truly believe that we serve a God worth dying for!

Appreciation is expressed to our friend Solomon Dinakaran, Whitefield, India, for his help in gathering information for this testimony.

2

BE STILL AND KNOW

joyce williams

Be still, and know that I am God.
—Ps. 46:10

Our little granddaughter Lauren Beth is a bundle of energy. We're enjoying (I think) the "terrific twos." Two of her favorite words are "No!" and "Mine!" She's still under construction—as is her Grammy.

Now that I'm advancing into my 60s, I find that keeping up with her is a feat of endurance! I understand the desire of Sarah, Abraham's wife, to be a mother. But can you imagine giving birth at 90—nighttime feedings, potty training, and chasing a toddler? No wonder she laughed! Was there a touch of hysteria there?

But every so often I find Lauren Beth sitting in the middle of the floor with a favorite book open as she "reads" it. It's her "quiet time."

May I be very honest and confess that being still is not easy for me? With my Type A personality, I'm usually on my way to the next project without finishing the last one! So quiet reflection and introspection are things I accomplish deliberately and methodically.

Don't get me wrong. I love my quiet times with the Lord. I've found the best time to get alone with Him is about 4:00 A.M. No one calls, the doorbell doesn't ring, and my computer doesn't announce, "You've got mail!" So I can truly listen for that still, small voice that renews and restores like nothing else.

The hectic, intense pace of ministry living can rob us of top-quality quiet time with the Lord regardless of our personality types. Since prayer and Bible study are not things we have to punch the clock to accomplish, they can be relegated to the back burner if we're not careful.

There are times when the Lord gets our attention through a crisis or defining moment and then enfolds us in a special embrace. Those divine hugs are watermark times that bless our lives.

I had one of those heavenly pauses on the Friday before Labor Day 1997. We were winding down pastoral ministry. Gene had pastored our last church for more than 26 years, with more than 47 total years of pastoring altogether. But he had reached that magical 65th birthday, and there were some questions about retirement time. Things were uneasy.

Also, my daughter Beth, who lived 1,000 miles away, was quite ill with a lupus flare-up. I had been back for several visits, but she was still so sick.

My fall speaking schedule was intense, so I had lots of preparation to do. This was in addition to the regular church schedule of ministries, services, activities, special events, and so on.

Plus, company was coming to stay with us for several days.

I had to make sure the house was clean, the beds were made, and the meals were planned. You know the routine. I was on major overload.

Finally, about two o'clock that Friday, I said some of what may be our Father's favorite words to hear: "I can't do this!" I picked up my Bible and headed around the lake behind our house to the prairie filled with golden sunflowers. No one was in sight.

Tears filled my eyes as I asked, *Father, would you please help me? This is just too hard.* I sat down on a grassy spot, opened my Bible, and began to read special highlighted passages. My heart paused when I read, "Be still, and know that I am God" (Ps. 46:10). It touched me as though I were reading it for the first time.

Forgetting everything else I had to do, I just sat there and basked in the quietude of that divine appointment. My Father had been trying for weeks to get my undivided attention. I had just been too busy to stop and listen. As He surrounded me with His presence, I felt the weary mantle slip from my shoulders as I shifted my burdens to Him. The minutes ticked away unnoticed as He whispered sweet promises to my heart.

Finally it was time to go. As I stood and brushed off my jeans, I looked at that sea of sunflowers. A gentle breeze caressed them, and it seemed as though they nodded in affirmation of His message: *God will take care of you and yours.*

So years later on another very intense ministry day, I thought about Lauren Beth. If an active toddler can settle down for quiet times, surely Grammy could follow her example.

And I took my favorite Book and headed back to the prairie.

Prayer: *Thank you, Father, for your patience and enfolding love.*

Thought for the Day: When asked what happens when she prays, Mother Teresa responded, "I listen." When asked what God does, she said, "He listens."

3 WAIT—DON'T WORRY

joyce baggott

Don't worry about anything; pray about everything. Tell God your needs and don't forget to thank Him for His answers. If you do this, you will experience God's peace, which is far more wonderful than the human mind can understand.
—Phil. 4:6-7, TLB

I was devastated with heaviness as I mentally rehearsed what the doctors had told me that day at the hospital in Columbia, South Carolina. Barney, my husband, had been diagnosed with an unspecified disease and had only six to nine months to live! The horrifying disease was attacking his lungs and other body tissues.

My mind was reeling with thoughts of not only losing Barney but all I would have to face if I were left alone with Paula and Julie, our two little girls. Our world was crumbling.

Since we had been in ministry all our married lives, we didn't own our home. We were young, so it had been impossible to save for the future as we had hoped. Now it seemed that I was facing that future by myself.

The doctors didn't want Barney to know how serious his condition was. So they asked me not to share this shocking news with our church or family. His parents were both heart patients. Their fragile health could not withstand the emotional trauma that might be triggered. My mother had passed away when I was 22. My father had remarried and moved far away near his new wife's family. Although he and I communicated infrequently, I did let him know what was going on.

For two weeks I took Paula and Julie to stay with a friend every day. Then I went to the hospital to sit with Barney. His fever was so high that sometimes he didn't even know me. My anxious heart throbbed with the anguish of the unknown. I felt powerless. There was nothing I could do to help him but pray. As I agonized over the impending major life changes, I wallowed in worry about Barney's condition, our girls, and our future.

Two nights before Barney was released from the hospital, I was reading Phil. 4:6-7 in *The Living Bible*. I realized I was spending precious time worrying and wasn't trusting God for my family's situation. After all, He knew what was going on far better than I.

That night I made a major commitment that with God's help I would not worry about *anything*. That sounds impossible, but anytime I feel myself leaning that way, I quote the Scripture verses God gave me that night.

I'm not going to tell you that I don't experience great concern about things, because I do. But God has revealed to me that when I have no control over a situation, worry is the useless, time-consuming tool of the devil.

A few days later, I took our two girls to my friend's home and headed to the hospital to get Barney. When I walked into his room, the doctors were there with him. Barney was ready to go. But the doctors told me to sit down because they had some new information. Fearfully, I perched on the edge of a chair.

They shared the whole scenario with us. They had misdiagnosed Barney's disease. They said it was identical to cancer but was not malignant. Barney was going to recover. The death sentence was lifted!

Wow! I never knew two minutes of conversation could have such a life-changing impact. I took a deep breath. "Elated" is not a strong-enough word to describe my feelings at that moment! God had been right there with us through it all.

God's Word is very quick and powerful. The promises He gave me were exactly what I needed to get me through that traumatic life experience. They continue to undergird my continuing day-to-day walk with Him. Many years have passed since that event. I can truthfully say that my faith has not wavered. Although we have weathered many more crises—some life-threatening—I can truly leave worry behind. Waiting on the Lord is the key.

And in waiting, not worrying, I totally relinquish control to my powerful Lord and Savior.

Prayer: *Thank you, Lord, for teaching me to relinquish control. For it's in my quiet times of stillness that you confirm your peace in my heart.*

Thought for the Day: Simple faith can remove the dense veil that sometimes seems to separate us from the face of God. Faith and trust go hand in hand. We must learn not to worry about *anything*. Instead, we must wait on Him.

4

A SAFE PLACE

sheila bird

My gracious favor is all you need.
My power works best in your weakness.
—2 Cor. 12:9, NLT

As a ministry wife, are you ever faced with questions like "Where is my safe place?" "Where do I go when life brings more than I can bear?" "Who can I talk with?" Let's face it—ministry life comes with many obstacles in our relationships with our spouses, children, church families, employers, and coworkers.

Obviously we must turn to the Lord. But in those times when we're silent because we have no words to pray, we're promised that the Holy Spirit intercedes for us. (See Rom. 8:26.) In those times God has taught me that what matters is the fact that His grace is sufficient for whatever comes.

We're in pretty good company. Paul felt the same way about some things in his life. Regarding what he called "a thorn in my flesh," he wrote,

> Three different times I begged the Lord to take it away. Each time he said, "My gracious favor is all you need. My

power works best in your weakness." So now I am glad to boast about my weaknesses, so that the power of Christ may work through me. Since I know it is all for Christ's good, I am quite content with my weaknesses and with insults, hardships, persecutions, and calamities. For when I am weak, then I am strong *(2 Cor. 12:8-10, NLT)*.

Isn't it true that many times it's our weakness that perpetuates our heartache? Why don't we run to Jesus and let Him hold us? We've all seen the pictures of the children clambering up onto Jesus' lap just to feel His arms of love around them. Why are we so afraid to go there ourselves? We read in Luke 18:15-17:

One day some parents brought their little children to Jesus so he could touch them and bless them, but the disciples told them not to bother him. Then Jesus called for the children and said to the disciples, "Let the children come to me. Don't stop them! For the Kingdom of God belongs to such as these. I assure you, anyone who doesn't have their kind of faith will never get into the Kingdom of God" (NLT).

Many times we don't want to bother the Lord with our cares—especially when we feel responsible for them. God has taught me to crawl into His lap like a little child, wrap my arms around His neck, and find safely and rest there as I let Him enfold me in His boundless love. In times when there's not much left of me, I've learned to truly let Him love me. I know I'm not bothering Him when I feel His comfort, love, peace, and companionship, and grace fills every fiber of my being.

Does the loneliness dissipate? Somewhat. Do the challenging relationships, circumstances, and bills go away? Not necessarily! Do I always keep my mouth shut when I should? Of course not! Does life have new strength? Absolutely! Why? Because God is God, and Christ says He's all I need.

This comfort challenges me to press daily toward eternity to finish this race on earth with as few skinned knees, broken arms, and amputations as possible. I find I must focus, refocus, and stumble to my heavenly prize one day, one moment, one second at a time. It's His strength, grace, and loving care that encourage me to take one more step.

I'm so thankful our Father sees me and loves me as I am. I picture Him standing there waiting for me with open arms, because I've learned to accept His comfort in this life. He's applauding and cheering for me along with all the other saints, waiting for me to cross the finish line, waiting to welcome me into my eternal home. I can't wait to hear Him say, "Well done, my good and faithful servant," and to see the smile on His face as He picks me up, throws me into the air, and says, "You did it!"

We must grab onto these words of hope today, keeping our eyes fixed on Jesus as we run our race of faith. Regardless of what life brings, we must keep pressing on with the dignity and grace that only He can provide.

Prayer: *Thank you, Father, that your arms are always open.*

Thought for the Day: An ordinary broken life entrusted to a loving Heavenly Father can be mended by His tender care.

5 A FORGIVEN FORGIVER

cindy blasdel

You have heard that it was said to the people long ago,
"Do not murder, and anyone who murders will be subject to
judgment." But I tell you that anyone who is angry
with his brother will be subject to judgment.
—Matt. 5:21-22

Our senior pastor was preaching through the Book of Matthew. After the third week in chapter 5 and hearing him talk at considerable length about forgiveness, I jokingly told him I wasn't going to come back if he spoke on it again. It took a long time for my heart to soften enough that God could genuinely talk to me.

Several years earlier we had moved to our present church from a city I loved dearly. I had many close friends there and was involved in two Moms in Touch groups in my neighborhood. I loved my piano students, some of whom I had taught for up to 10 years. I was very involved in the music ministry at our church, where my husband had been minister of music for more than 11 years. Then things changed to the point that we could no longer stay. Our family was devastated. Frankly, I was very angry.

Our oldest child was a senior in high school when all this happened, so we decided he would stay there for his last semester. Steve began work at his new ministry position November 1. The kids and I moved the week of Christmas. The weather matched my mood—freezing rain. I had so much bitterness in my heart.

I spent the first month unpacking, painting rooms, and crying every day. I yearned to hear my phone ring. I wanted piano students. I wanted friends. As a high-energy person, I wanted something—anything—to do!

Then a dear lady came to me and said, "If you need a friend, I'll be that person," and somehow I took her at her word. I started teaching piano again. I got involved at our new church. I was asked to teach a music class at the college where I had received my undergraduate degree. After much prayer and with considerable terror, I took the position. What a delight it was! I suddenly had several things I loved to do.

But when I thought of our former church, it was with bitterness. After those sermons from Matthew, God continued to be the "Hound of heaven" as He examined the ugliness in my heart.

Finally I was able to say to God, "I've sinned. Please forgive me." I thought I was finished, but He would not let me off the hook that easily. I began to realize that I needed to write letters asking for forgiveness from the people I had sinned against. Once again, that took quite a while.

But God is faithful. He continued loving me and bringing verses to my mind. One was 1 John 4:20-21: "If anyone says, 'I love God,' yet hates his brother, he is a liar. For anyone who does not love his brother, whom he has seen, cannot love God, whom he has not seen. And he has given us this command: Whoever loves God must also love his brother."

So I wrote letters asking forgiveness for my attitude and actions. I was able to say to my friends in that city, "It's over. God is healing my emotions."

Soon after we moved here, my mother needed assisted living, and we moved her nearby. It was an honor to serve her the last seven years of her life as her health deteriorated, and I was so glad I was able to be with her the final days of her life.

This is the city where my husband grew up, and we've been reconnecting with family members. Our oldest son met his wife in our church, our other children have made wonderful friends, and so have I. I love teaching at the college and am fulfilled in many ways. I not only teach but get to mentor and mother the students as well.

God is so merciful. It's refreshing to be clean before Him! I have been forgiven so I can in turn forgive.

Prayer: *Thank you, Father, for not judging me as I judged others. I'm so thankful you didn't give up on me.*

Thought for the Day: We serve the God of second chances.

6 WINGS FOR MINISTRY

sally bond

She speaks with wisdom, and faithful instruction
is on her tongue.
—Prov. 31:26

Her name was Velda. She was a seasoned pastor's wife when she and her husband joined our pastoral team. My husband and I were young—too young—to pastor a church with 1,000 in attendance. Jim was 29, and I was 25.

I was an insecure young pastor's wife, and my feelings of inadequacy were fed by my healthy respect and admiration for women who had preceded us in ministry at that church. Also, I didn't play the piano, and I knew that was expected of ministers' wives at that time. I didn't have a specific ministry in the church. I found lots of things I couldn't do, and I often focused on my inabilities. I was overwhelmed by the challenges. Then Velda came into my life.

Velda gave me my wings for ministry. She taught me that not all ministry wives fit the stereotypical role of pastor's wife. She moved alongside me and affirmed qualities of character that could become strengths in ministry. She saw things in me that I didn't see in myself. When she heard a favorable comment about me—perhaps some little thing I did behind the scenes—she passed it on to me with a comment like "Oh, Sally—don't you see how special it is to have the privilege to encourage!" While I had been looking to excel in public performance, she affirmed my natural desires or God-given talents. Velda understood that fulfillment comes by developing into the person God created me to be.

She knew I had a fun-loving personality and would enjoy having people over. Although I liked to be with people, I was reluctant to entertain in our home, because I felt I couldn't do it in a style that would complement Jim's ministry. Velda began to invite us to her home when she entertained. She asked me to help in the kitchen, discussed menus with me, shared recipes, and always talked to her guests in a gracious way.

I observed that Velda really listened to people when they were engaged in conversation. It always amazed me that she remembered important information about each person that showed her sincere interest in him or her. She was modeling for me—showing me how—and was making it so much fun.

Everyone who knew Velda realized she was a woman who had been with God. I wanted to be just like her. One day I said to her, "I wish I was like you. You have such an understanding of the Word. Your prayers are so meaningful and helpful."

She replied, "Sally, it just takes time. Give God a chance to do His work in your life." When she went to the altar to pray with someone, I often knelt nearby so I could better understand how to help seekers.

What a legacy Velda Hartley left in my heart! I've tried to perpetuate her ministry by showing the same spirit of love, care, kindness, wisdom, and understanding. Now I love moving alongside young ministry wives with hugs, affirmation, and words of encouragement.

My prayer is that they, too, will learn to spread their wings and soar into the full potential that God has planned for their ministries.

Prayer: *Thank you, Father, for sending someone to give me wings to soar for you. Help me be an encourager to ministry wives who need to be affirmed and uplifted by you today.*

Thought for the Day: Words of wisdom and encouragement are investments in the Bank of Heaven. The dividends are eternal.

7

FRUITS OF OUR LABORS

vonette bright

Always give yourselves fully to the work of the Lord,
because you know that your labor in the Lord is not in vain.
—I Cor. 15:58

We ministry wives never know exactly what the Lord will do for us each day. Sometimes we get to clip an unexpected coupon as a result of ministry from years earlier.

I still remember that beautiful spring day in North Carolina. To my amazement, I had been invited to be the commencement speaker for a Christian high school. Many times I feared that those inviting me really wanted Bill, and if he wasn't available, they took me. But this time they truly wanted me.

My notes were tucked into my Bible when I arrived at the auditorium. I was escorted to my designated place on the platform. As I looked around, I felt honored to be sitting with the faculty members and others who had given their lives to teaching those fine young people about our Lord. It was exciting to see the radiating love of Christ that permeated the auditorium as proud parents beamed and excited students took their places.

We held our breath as we watched the valedictorian walk up the steps to deliver her speech in high-heeled shoes that orthopedists warn us not to wear. She was beautiful. Her flowing brown hair shone beneath her mortarboard. It was exciting to watch her as she spoke gracefully and enthusiastically. She had great poise and presence that exuded the love of God.

To my amazement, she paused and turned to look at me and began to express her gratitude that I was part of her graduation ceremonies. She said, "I want you to know the timeliness of your presence at my graduation. My mother and father both received Christ while on college campuses through the ministry of Campus Crusade for Christ. They met at a student conference at Arrowhead Springs. Now here I am, the next generation, living out the legacy of faith."

I was so touched by her testimony. Many times we never see the fruits of our labors. What a blessing to see the tangible return on the investment we made many years prior to that day! It was a joyous occasion to witness a second-generation believer with her life ahead of her, eager to find all that God had planned for her.

God had given my husband, Bill, a great vision many years earlier. The rewards for all the years and all the work Bill and I, along with our wonderful staff, had been privileged to do were encapsulated in this beautiful young lady.

As she returned to her address, she challenged the other students to treasure the blessings of the Christian education they had received. She encouraged them to cherish their friendships with each other and always to hold to the values that had been instilled in them by their parents and teachers. Her face radiated with her contagious enthusiasm and love for Jesus.

When it was time for me to present my message, I breathed a silent prayer. I wanted so much to be used by the Holy Spirit to infuse lasting joy and excitement about our Lord into the hearts of those dear students.

As I shared with them, I was overshadowed by the joy of tangibly reaping some of the seeds we had planted that had been harvested in that precious young lady.

Our Lord promised that if we fully surrender our lives to Him, our labors will not be in vain. I pray those students saw that day a visible manifestation of what God can do when we totally give our hearts to Him.

As I remember that wonderful day, my heart sends out a virtual hug to that sweet young woman, wherever she may be. May all who encounter her on life's pathway share the beautiful fruits of her faith.

Prayer: *Thank you, Lord, for the eternal treasures we reap by investing in the kingdom of heaven.*

Thought for the Day: The fruit from the harvest of souls is sweet indeed.

8

THE GOD WHO WILL NOT FORGET YOU

jennifer buettner

I will not forget you! See, I have engraved you on the palms of my hands; your walls are ever before me.
—Isa. 49:15-16

We were in the process of relocating our church and building a new plant in 2001. God had been incredibly good to us. In 1993 my husband, Harlan, and I had begun to pastor a church that averaged 275 in attendance. We rolled up our sleeves and went to work. God blessed us with many miracles, and the church soon grew to more than 500 people.

In 1999 we knew it was time to relocate. Without advertising, our church building sold even though five others were on the market. A person stepped forward and purchased new land on which we could build. Miracles just kept happening.

During the transition our congregation worshiped in a 10-screen movie theater that was painted pink! Could God bless a church that met in a pink movie theater? Did He ever!

Our people worked hard. We had three 20-foot trailers loaded with equipment that had to be set up every Sunday morning. At 5:30 A.M. we brought in sound systems, lighting, staging, musical instruments, media, everything we needed for church. We set up our nursery in the game room, and the snack bar became our welcome center. Sunday School classes met in the smaller theaters, and the worship center occupied the largest theater. By 7:30 on Sunday mornings we were doing sound checks and choir rehearsal. At 8:00 we were ready to go. The first worship service began at 8:30.

What great services! Both were full of energy and excitement. People who never would have darkened the door of a traditional church came.

We had to be out of the theater by 12:30 P.M., when the matinees began. Sometimes during our altar call in the second service we could smell the popcorn the theater employees were popping. It took us about 45 minutes to tear down, load the trailers, and get away.

Our hardworking church members were excited about starting construction on the new building. We hoped to be in it by the summer of 2002.

But then came September 11, 2001. The entire nation suddenly went into shock and mourning. However, as sad as we were, we didn't expect our Midwestern city to be greatly affected. We were wrong! The airline industry was devastated by the tragedy, and that impacted our people tremendously. In a city known as "the air capital of the world," the aircraft manufacturing plants are major employers.

We had just begun construction. Our city was the second hardest-hit economically by September 11. It affected our church financially, because our people simply weren't able to give as much as they wanted due to layoffs and other factors. Harlan and I both had trouble sleeping.

I remember crying out to God, *What are we going to do? We've stepped out in faith believing this was your will, shown by all the miracles. Now this! Please show us what to do.* I began to stress obsessively, thinking about our crisis all the time. What if God didn't come through? What if we didn't have the financial miracle we needed?

Then one day as I was having my devotions, God led me to Isaiah 49. I read the verse that says, "But Zion said, 'The LORD has forsaken me, the Lord has forgotten me'" (v. 14). I thought, *I feel just like that.* But I went on to read the Lord's answer: "Can a mother forget the baby at her breast and have no compassion on the child she has borne? Though she may forget, I will not forget you! See, I have engraved you on the palms of my hands; your walls are ever before me" (vv. 15-16).

What incredible comfort that was to me! God will never forget or forsake us. I remember thinking about the phrase "See, I have engraved you on the palms of my hands." There's no way to forget anyone engraved on your palms. He or she is always there!

Did things get easy after that? Not immediately. But each time I began to worry and wonder if God knew about our situation, I remembered this promise. And He got us through.

I rejoice that our names are branded on the hands that guide us.

Prayer: *Thank you, Father, for never leaving or forsaking us, especially during tough times.*

Thought for the Day: As we follow God's will, we may go through some dark times—but we're never without *Son*light.

9

I DON'T
KNOW
WHO I AM

myrna buhler

He calls his own sheep by name and leads them out.
—John 10:3

I have chatted with many ministry wives over the years, and I often ask them, "Do you sometimes feel you don't know who you are anymore?" Many times the answer is a resounding "Yes!" This seems to be especially true for women who have not taken jobs outside their homes and are full-time ministry partners with their husbands. These women are strongly gifted, talented, and educated and have responded to God's call to be ministry partners.

I'm one of them, and for the most part I love who I am and what I do. It is a joy to be in a supporting role in my husband, Brian's, ministry. Being a pastor these days is not an easy job, so I love making our home a safe place for Brian to live and be. I enjoy the ministries in which I have taken leadership in the church. I believe I am in the place God wants me.

After being introduced as "the pastor's wife" for about the fifth time with no mention of my name, however, I could feel that my value is connected only to Brian and what he does. Another example is when I am asked what I do and it comes out that my husband is a pastor. That seems to be all I need to say. Sometimes I am asked questions only about my husband and what he does and likes. It would be easy to feel that my only value is because of his ministry.

But the toughest questions are those asked about what I like to do or what my passions are aside from church, and I find that everything meaningful to me is connected to my husband, my family, or the church. Suddenly I feel that I don't even know who I am anymore and that I have been swallowed by my husband's life.

But I know where to go to find out who I am. Jesus doesn't call me Brian's wife or Grady's, Charlie's, or Annie's mom. I'm not just Carly's and Becky's mother-in-law. I'm not just a sister or a church leader. John 10:3 says that Jesus calls each of us by name. He calls me Myrna.

I have realized that I love to be called by name, just my name. When someone calls my name, doesn't he or she usually want me for something? So what does Jesus want when He calls me by name? I believe He wants me to come and dine, come and drink, come and sit, come and listen, come and be just *me*.

John also says that Jesus is the Good Shepherd and that He knows His sheep and His sheep know Him. I am one of His sheep, and not only does He know my name—He knows *me*. David wrote, "O LORD, you have searched me and you know me" (Ps. 139:1).

When I forget who I am, I go to the One who knows me inside and out. He understands all the "stuff" about being a pastor's wife and how I live in a fishbowl and all of the realities and expectations I live with. He understands about people wanting to get close to me so I can communicate certain things to my husband. He understands that I am invited to some homes because it looks good to have the pastor's wife there. He understands when women don't invite me to go shopping because they think it might not be spiritual enough.

But when I answer His call to come, I know I can truly be me. I don't have to pretend, and I don't have to be careful about what I say or how I say it. I can share my feelings, I can express my pain and hurt, and I can express my excitement and joy because of something the Lord has provided because I am the pastor's wife. I don't even have to get dressed if I don't want to. He knows my name, and He knows me . . . just me.

Prayer: *Lord, help me remember that it doesn't matter what I am but whose I am. Thank you.*

Thought for the Day: When we forget who we are, Jesus whispers, "I am yours and you are mine." Listen for your name.

10

LAMBS INTO THE FOLD

joyce williams

*I will contend with those who contend with you,
and your children I will save.*
—Isa. 49:25

It happened again today. As I was folding the laundry, I realized two socks were missing. Friends were coming to visit, and I had a jillion things to do. How irritating! Where do all those socks go? Surely there must be a huge sock mountain somewhere!

In the broader context of things, I know the mysterious disappearance of socks is not really a big deal. But in ministry most days are crammed to the brim. So "the case of the missing socks" became another irritant to add to a growing list.

Determined to find them, I carefully sorted through the laundry and rechecked the washer and dryer. Not there! This had become a great mystery. The sleuth in me wanted to find those socks.

As I continued to search, I reflected on a conversation I had had the previous weekend with a brokenhearted pastor's wife. Gene and I had been retreat speakers for clergy couples.

It didn't take long for us to realize that many of those couples were hurting.

In working with our Shepherds' Fold Ministries for clergy families, Gene and I have found the most pervasive heartache many ministry couples share is that of children who are away from the Lord. That mother's lamb was lost.

In her deep distress she tearfully confided that their son was destroying himself with drugs and gambling. Tears spilled from her eyes as she shared her heartache. Her anguished words echoed many others as she cried, "He is so lost! What could we have done differently? What can we do for him? Is there any hope?"

After listening for a while, I shared a promise the Lord had given to me years earlier from Isa. 49:25: "I will contend with those who contend with you, and your children I will save." Wrapping my arm around her shoulder, I prayed with her.

Then I went on to remind her that the Holy Spirit, the Hound of Heaven, is persistently pursuing our loved ones. What a comfort it is to picture Him in loving pursuit of our lambs, regardless of how far they may roam into the far country!

With tears streaming down both our faces, we agreed together to pray presumptively, anticipating the day when her lamb will come home. I tucked a small porcelain lamb into her hand from the stash I keep on hand so she could take it as a tangible reminder that our Good Shepherd cares. I reminded her that He never gives up and that He is always in pursuit. The Hound of Heaven can go where we cannot go, be what we cannot be, do what we cannot do, and say what we cannot say. As she walked away clutching her little figurine, I saw a faint flicker of fresh hope.

Tucking away the last laundry item, I found my heart warmed as I reflected on the patience of our faithful Good Shepherd. He's not satisfied with 99 but goes after the last lost one. (See Luke 15:1-7.) As I stood there, I could picture our lambs running into His tender, loving, outstretched arms. What a day that will be!

Well, my persistence finally paid off. I finally found one of the prodigal socks tucked into the corner of a fitted sheet. It was satisfying to match it with its mate and put it into the appropriate color-coordinated slot in the drawer.

How comforting to realize that the Hound of Heaven pursues our lambs into the darkest corners of their lives! Our Lord has reserved a special place custom-designed for them in His fold. And when they do return from their far-country wanderings, a party in heaven takes place in their honor! Jesus told us about that in Luke 15:10: "I tell you, there is rejoicing in the presence of the angels of God over one sinner who repents."

Our comfort, prayer, and hope is that someday we'll rejoice together with the heavenly realm when our lambs are back in the fold.

Prayer: *Thank you, our Good Shepherd, for pursuing all our lambs and for the everlasting hope you give us. We rejoice together in anticipation of the coming celebration.*

Thought for the Day: As our Good Shepherd, you know just where our lambs are when they're out of the fold. Please hold them close, keep them safe, and bring them home. We trust your schedule, not ours.

11  MOVING INTO THE NEIGHBORHOOD

rachael crabb

> *The Word became flesh and blood,*
> *and moved into the neighborhood.*
> —John 1:14, TM

When our boys were small, ages one and three, we were in our early years of ministry and had just been transferred to a different state, a very different climate, and a brand-new and totally unfamiliar community. After several months of apartment living and househunting, we settled into a neighborhood and began what was to be our second home-building project in a long line of moves.

Only problem was, I didn't want to live on a corner lot—too accessible to dogs, trespassers, and noise—but it was one of the few remaining lots in the family-oriented neighborhood we could afford. Staying in the house, hidden away with two small boys, was just fine with me. After all, I wasn't feeling very sociable. But it wasn't fine with God. He had other plans.

One day a neighbor lady from across the street came to welcome us to the neighborhood with this statement: "Someone told me you guys are Christians, and I want you to know that you're an answer to my prayer for God to put a Christian family on this corner lot." In my heart I muttered, *Oh, great—it's your fault I'm living here!* Yet because of this woman's kindness, I found my heart slowly softening toward my new neighbors.

From that point on, living on that corner became the opportunity for God to become flesh and move into the neighborhood. What an exciting ministry we had during those years!

I fondly remember those New Year's Eve progressive dinners that concluded with a watch night service at our church. I received thank-you notes from the neighbors who came, saying what a great time they had without getting drunk.

There were many Friendship Bible Coffees (Stonecroft Ministries) with sometimes as many as 16 women and their children in my home. One neighbor who had never attended our study was hospitalized in another state for a brain tumor operation. Our group sent a card to her every week. When she was able to return to her home, she insisted the study be held at her house! Bible studies for couples were held in the home of one of the families who came to a saving faith in Christ Jesus and joined our church fellowship. Through them God moved even farther into the neighborhood I had come to love.

Although I had felt *dislocated,* it became clear that God had simply *relocated* me for purposes I now see in hindsight, and I'm grateful. That's often the way He works with ministry wives.

We ask once again today, "And who is my neighbor?" (Luke 10:29). Our neighbor is the person right next to us or across the street. Jesus challenged us, "Love your neighbor as yourself" (Matt. 19:19). And we need to stay focused on the fact that our Heavenly Father always places us right where He can use us.

I wish I were sitting with you right now to hear whether that's your experience as well. I bet it is. What a blessed privilege it is that our Heavenly Father uses those of us who are believers to infiltrate our neighborhoods with His love!

Prayer: *Dear Triune God, thank you for the opportunity we have in our neighborhoods to represent you in the flesh.*

Thought for the Day: We must think about what our neighbors will look like in their eternal state. God is always ready to use each one of us to make a difference that will change their lives forever!

12 BIBLE SCHOOL AT THE CITY DUMP

betty daily

*You will be my witnesses in Jerusalem, and in all
Judea and Samaria, and to the ends of the earth.*
—Acts 1:8

From my early childhood, missions pulled at my heart. I
yearned to be involved, but I never felt a specific call to a particular country or people.

Shortly after Bob and I were married, we began to pastor
our first church. I thought my calling to the mission field would
be satisfied through ministry in our local churches. For the
most part, I really enjoyed the multiple challenges and rewards
of those 35 years of pastoral ministry in my "Jerusalem, Judea,
and Samaria" assignments. But that tug toward world missions
remained deep within my heart.

About 25 years ago I heard about short-term missions opportunities. My first Work and Witness trip to the Dominican
Republic was truly the beginning fulfillment of my childhood

yearning. Finally I actually ministered "to the ends of the earth." I was permanently infected with a lasting commitment to make myself available to participate in missions the Lord would lead me to. Since then, I've had the awesome privilege to be part of 25 mission trips working with some of God's great missionary giants in 12 countries.

When the call came in 2004 about the possibility of going to Ethiopia, I had to be sure of God's plans for me. As I prayed, I asked the Lord to make it clear if that was a trip He wanted me to make. The travel would be very long and difficult. I wasn't sure there was anything I could do as part of the team that would truly be helpful.

A few days later, a friend called to discuss Ethiopia once again. As we talked about the plans, the Lord spoke to me and asked if I would be willing to go. My answer was a joyful and immediate "Yes!" And just like that, my name was added to the team's list.

We were all excited when we arrived in Ethiopia. It was amazing to watch the Lord go ahead of us and prepare the way as He had done in so many previous situations.

One evening we ran out of gas after showing the *JESUS* film in an Islamic village more than three hours from our city. It was dark, and there was no gas station in sight. Miraculously, the people began to bring gas in cans, and they poured fuel into our vehicle. To this day we don't know how that happened except to say that God provided. We received just enough fuel to get to the place we were staying. Our Good Shepherd was always present, guarding and guiding us.

We ladies worked at the job site in the mornings, and in the afternoons we taught Bible school in what was called a "bush church" located at the city dump. The conditions were deplorable—about the worst I have ever experienced.

As we ministered there each day, our hearts were deeply touched by the overwhelming needs. We did what we could, but there was no way to provide for all their desperate situations. What we did provide them was hope by sharing the love of Jesus.

As we hugged the precious children who were so sad, lonely, and forlorn, we tried to *be* Jesus to them in other ways as well. It was worth everything to see those hopeless eyes light up with the truth as we watched many of them give their hearts to the Lord. Smiles spread across their faces as hope filled their lives for the first time. It seemed I glimpsed a reflection of God's childhood call on my life in their response.

I left part of my heart with those precious children. My prayer today is that the beauty of Jesus will continue to permeate the debris of that city dump.

I can hardly wait to return next year to see how the beauty of Jesus is continuing to emerge from the ashes of despair.

Prayer: *Father, may we always be Jesus to those around us—whether at home or on a far-flung mission field.*

Thought for the Day: It's a blessing to see the hope of the Rose of Sharon blossom in the most unlikely places.

13

RELEASE
AND WAIT

susan dillow

I wait for the LORD, my soul waits, and in his word I put my hope.
—Ps. 130:5

The Lord often has to do a number on me when it comes to waiting. I'm a get-busy-and-get-the-job-finished type of person. So I find it difficult to slow down when there are things still to be done. When I see a problem, it's my nature to interfere and fix it, even when I should wait. This is especially true where my children are concerned.

Not long ago I watched as Tim and Danae, our younger son and daughter-in-law, praised God while singing with their church's worship team on a Sunday morning. I thought about our grandson Camden, who was in the nursery learning about Jesus. My eyes filled with tears and my heart welled with joy as I was reminded that our knowing, omnipresent, loving Lord truly answers prayer in His time and in His way.

I reflected back to a few years earlier when Tim and Danae had gone through some very difficult days during their dating relationship. For the first time in my life I knew how "heart-ache" felt. I was living out the verse "Pray without ceasing" (1 Thess. 5:17, KJV) and spending much time in God's Word.

I confess that I was discouraged and worried constantly because I could not see God working.

Then one crisp October morning, I went to my prayer closet—a worn recliner beside an end table covered with my Bible and study books—to spend time with the Lord. From that vantage point I can enjoy the view of the woods behind our home. I had just finished a Bible study on relinquishment.

It was time for prayer. I began again, as I had throughout the weeks and months, praying for God's answers and telling Him what to do. Rather than taking time to wait and listen, I was busy giving Him advice.

Suddenly I stopped praying as I felt the Holy Spirit speaking to my heart. It seemed He was saying, *Susan, stop and listen to me!* In those quiet moments His almost audible voice seemed to say, *What will you do if I don't answer the way you think I should? Are you willing to let go, hands down, and allow me to do my work in Tim's life?*

The minutes moved into an hour as I waited quietly before Him. It's not easy for a mother to let go and totally relinquish her children to God. We had dedicated Tim to God when he was a baby and had prayed over him his entire life. But totally letting go of my son was another brand-new commitment on my part.

I suddenly realized my stubbornness in not letting go so God could work. In that moment my heart cried out, *O God, please forgive me. Regardless of the outcome, I will praise you, I will have faith in you, I will always love you. You will always occupy first place in my life.*

The peace I had sought for weeks swept over me as His sweet, quiet presence ministered to my heart. I felt the calming reassurance that He was working and would answer prayer in His time and His perfect way.

The very next day Tim called, and as he spoke about trusting God, I knew God was at work. When we finished talking, I praised God and thanked Him. I told God I would rejoice in each baby step Tim and Danae took as He continued to work in their lives.

Tim called a few days later to tell us that he and Danae had found a loving church family and a caring pastor who was ministering to them. I began to realize God had been working all the time. I had been so busy trying to tell Him how I thought the problem should be solved that I had failed to listen and wait for His answers.

The rest of the story is about a young family—Tim, Danae, Camden, and Lane, who was on the way—living for the Lord and testifying to His goodness to them. God has supplied good jobs, a wonderful church family, their own home, and two sets of loving, supportive parents.

Truly God rewards total obedience when we let go and trust Him.

Prayer: *Thank you for teaching me to release and wait. I totally commit, hands down, all that this day holds with family, friends, ministry, and work.*

Thought for the Day: God may not often be early, but He's always on time.

14 BEAUTY IN THE JOURNEY

denise franklin

For those who are righteous, the path is not steep and rough. You are a God of justice, and you smooth out the road ahead of them.
—Isa. 28:7, NLT

There was great excitement at our house early that evening as my husband, Kendall, and our nine-year-old son, Trevor, got our bikes ready for the trail. Water bottles were filled, tires were pumped up, and helmets were made ready. This would be the second time on the trail for Trevor, and it was the first time for Kendall and me. I could hardly wait to make this memory. Kendall's time is often taken up with church work and well-meaning people. We loaded everything and headed to the bike trail, organizing ourselves according to stamina— Kendall, Trevor, and then me.

As we neared the one-mile mark, Trevor looked back at me and asked, "How are you doing, Mom?"

Breathlessly I answered, "I'm just fine."

I kept telling myself, *Surely I can do this if Trevor can!* His little legs seemed so energetic, while my long legs seemed so heavy.

Each hill was a struggle, but the other side was an anticipated relief as we all coasted down.

Soon we came to the halfway point. There was a gazebo, a picnic table, and a map showing how far we had come and how far we had to go. We took a water break to catch our breath. Then I said, "Since this is a school night, we probably should turn back. Trevor needs to get to bed on time." Also, my seat was getting a little sore, and I knew the morning would probably bring other aches and pains.

With renewed energy Kendall led the way, and I brought up the rear as we headed back. I focused on reaching our destination while striving to keep my mouth shut to avoid bugs hitting my teeth. I noticed our pace had slowed somewhat and we—well, at least Trevor and I—were enjoying the scenery a little more.

Suddenly I heard Trevor groan. When I asked him what was wrong, he said breathlessly, "Look at that big hill ahead of us!" Always looking for a chance to teach our three boys what God can do in our daily situations, I told him to stop his bike for a minute. Then I said, "Look around you at the beautiful stream nestled in the green grass to our left and the gorgeous flowers to our right. Listen to the birds as they sing. Isn't this great? Trevor, focus on where you are right now. Don't worry about what's ahead of you."

Then it hit me. That's what *I* need to be doing! It was as though God were saying, *Denise, don't focus on all the what-ifs that wake you up at night. Focus on where I've placed you right now. Enjoy the blessings I'm giving you. Then when the time comes to ride up a big hill, you can be sure I'll give you the stamina to reach the top!*

Much to Trevor's happiness (and mine), when we got to the bottom of the hill we had a choice. We could either go to the right, which was up the hill, or to the left, which was straight ahead without a hill in sight. I think you know the route we chose!

So it is with all our what-ifs. Many times in ministry we encounter situations that cause us concern, and we must have God's strength to reach the top. But there are also many times we worry about events in the future that never take place.

That evening the lesson I was sure God was teaching Trevor—and me—was to *be still* and enjoy the beauty in our present surroundings, wherever that may be. Then when we're apprehensive about the future, we can remember that God is bigger than the highest mountain we may have to climb and stronger than any struggle we may encounter!

He's always on the trail with us—taking the lead if we let Him.

Prayer: *Thank you, Lord, for the lessons you teach me in the busyness of my daily activities.*

Thought for the Day: Don't spend your time worrying about events in the future that may never take place. Allow your Heavenly Father to lead you where He wants to take you—and enjoy the beauty along the way.

15

MY FIRST LOVE

kendra graham

I know your deeds, your hard work and your perseverance....
You have persevered and have endured hardships for my name,
and have not grown weary. Yet I hold this against you:
You have forsaken your first love.
—Rev. 2:2-4

I couldn't wait to get out of bed in the morning. I rushed to the bathroom, showered, and prayed that my mousse, hairspray, and teasing comb would come together in perfect harmony. Then I got dressed. I rushed to class, eager to see Wil, my love, and sit next to him.

We enjoyed many hours together, just talking. I absorbed every word, *really* listening—trying to understand who he was and where he was coming from. To be honest, it didn't matter if we said *anything*. Being next to each other was enough.

What fun to remember those early days! I *did* marry Wil—this fabulous love of mine—in June 1998. Today, however, with our third child due any moment, my early-morning routine is vastly different.

In those wonderful days of first being in love and then married, I was tuned in to every aspect of Wil's life. As I encouraged his dreams, I planned how I could fit into what he felt God wanted him to do. As a planner, I love to organize weeks and months ahead. Any little change in "the plan" is a major prayer event in my life.

When we were engaged, then married, and went on to seminary, the only thing Wil knew for sure was that he wasn't going to be a pastor. He thought God wanted him to teach or be a missionary. So much for our plans! God called Wil to preach! He's now well into his fourth year of pastoring a small church.

Wil had been preaching for about six months when a sweet lady approached me and asked what *I* did in the church. If I had been honest I would have said, "I hyperventilate!" I was a nurse, wife, and mother with a three-month-old baby. I hadn't adequately prepared to be a pastor's wife. I was too young to be a pastor's wife! I hadn't the time nor did I fit the profile. It hadn't been in our *plan*. *Wil* was the one who was called! I was so focused on him that I didn't properly think about what that meant for me. What *did* I do anyway?

I began to pray as never before. God told me to be still and wait. Great! Now when they asked, I could actually say "I *do* nothing!" The more I prayed, the more God answered, "Be still and wait."

Two years passed. We had two small babies, but God's answer remained the same. Then He led me to Rev. 2:2-7. I read it and listened to a message given by my husband's aunt, Anne Graham Lotz.

The church at Ephesus was great—a cutting-edge church for the times. The people were busy for God with every kind of ministry. God noticed their hard work and perseverance, but He had something against them. They had become too busy to sit at His feet. They had lost their first love.

I still remember my excitement for God as a new Christian. It was a lot like falling in love with Wil. I couldn't wait for my quiet times alone with my Lord, sitting at His feet, soaking in His Word. With the busyness of my life, I had little time to "be still." There was always so much to do.

Then it finally dawned on me. God was not expecting me to do ministry because I was a pastor's wife. Instead of just being busy doing ministry, I needed time to sit at His feet and love Him. The ministry God called me to would flow naturally from my worship of Him.

Finally, after two-and-one-half years of just loving God, He asked me to do something for Him! What a joy to do ministry—not for my husband, my church, or all the people who asked me what I *do*—but for my Lord.

And that's when I returned to my first love.

Prayer: *Lord, as ministry wives, may we always place you as our first love. Slow us down and give us patience to wait on you. Use us where you want us—not where we or others think we need to be.*

Thought for the Day: Hold tight to your first love by being still before Him. Then He will reveal His custom-designed ministry plan for you.

16

A CUP
OF COLD
LEMONADE

joyce williams

"The water I give them," he said, "becomes a perpetual spring
within them, watering them forever with eternal life."
—John 4:14, TLB

Shimmering blisters of Kansas sun bubbled in the blinding heat of the July Saturday noon. With the temperature nudging 100 degrees, it was a good day to be inside. But I was participating in one of my favorite duties as a pastor's wife.

Approximately 30 of us from 10 different churches and several denominations gathered on the sweltering pavement in downtown Wichita to prepare for a cookout for more than 100 very special people. Some of Wichita's homeless street people would be coming for their weekly lunch appointment.

For several years churches have united together to feed the needy and homeless on Saturdays. The line of tables stretched in the shade of the swaying cottonwoods reminded me of the Sunday dinners on the ground of my childhood.

As the aroma of grilling burgers and hotdogs flung fragrant fingers drifting along the city streets, people began to gather, calling greetings to acquaintances. Old friends teased each other as they waited patiently in line. Before long, they moved through the line with plates laden with burgers, hot dogs, potato salad, and even tossed salads splashed with ranch dressing. For whatever reason, we kept running out of hotdogs. As more came off the grill, it was worth another trip through the line to get one.

All of us, servers and guests, were a melting pot of personalities. Jack spoke fluent Spanish with our Hispanic friends. A young Vietnamese man's face brightened when he was handed a full plate, although he couldn't understand much of what was said. Another man had just gotten out of jail. There was an older man who could barely walk, and a young lady in a wheelchair.

With much practice and expertise, the servers dispensed food and cheery greetings and words of encouragement. We ranged from Betty, with her silvery curls circled by a headband, to six-year-old Ashley, whose red hair glistened in the sun as she handed out bananas. Many took an extra banana for the road.

It was a beautiful scene. There were no recriminations, no judgmental criticism, no sermonizing. From time to time our guests quietly drifted to Jack, Rick, or someone else and whispered their special needs. Pulling a tract or small Testament from a pocket, we were glad to point them to the One who is the answer.

Reverently, in that outdoor cathedral with branches swaying gently and grass growing underfoot, they softly prayed together. Everybody knew that we cared. But the primary message taught that day was the one being lived out in flesh and blood.

Our guests couldn't get enough to drink. Huge jugs of water and lemonade were quickly emptied—especially the lemonade. We kept refilling their big cups again and again. Marita handed her canteen to me. Unfortunately, I was momentarily distracted and splashed lemonade on the outside. She cried out in dismay, "You've ruined it! Now it will be sticky every time I touch it!" Realizing how valuable that container was to her, I painstakingly scrubbed the outside so that it would be as good as new.

It was obvious to us on that sweltering day that life had handed a lot of lemons to these unfortunate friends. I was reminded of the words of Jesus encouraging us to give a cup of cold water in His name.

As we filled their containers, our hope was that they would see something in us to give them hope. Maybe they would take the lemons of life and mix them with the sweetness of the Lord. Then they, too, could taste the fresh elixir of Jesus— the water of life—that lasts forever.

Later, as Marita was leaving, she turned to say, "Hey! Thanks for the lemonade—both inside and out!"

I replied, "Sure! And we want you to drink deeply of the sweet and living well that only peace with God can bring." She listened intently as I told her about Jesus.

I told her that although we ran out of lemonade on that hot day, the living water that comes from knowing Jesus is an everlasting well that never runs out. It fills body and soul—inside and out. I was blessed to get to pray with her. As she turned to leave, I said, "Remember—regardless of how hot it gets, your soul never has to thirst again!"

I pray she took away more than her lemonade canteen.

Prayer: *Father, may I always pour the living water of your love onto those around me.*

Thought for the Day: The perks of being a ministry wife are out of this world!

17

FIX YOUR EYES
karan gunter

Let us fix our eyes on Jesus, the author and perfecter of our faith.
—Heb. 12:2

It was a mountaintop experience—and I'm afraid of heights! I'm also afraid of speed and risk and dangerous adventure sports! We were in Vail, Colorado, 11,000 feet above sea level. Cottony clouds were scattered across a crystal-blue sky, and we could see for miles! The Rocky Mountains were at their best—soaring, snow-covered, and majestic. I could hardly believe I was actually standing up there—*way* up there.

As I waited for the rest of our church group, the question of how in the world I would get down crossed my mind. I had been assured there *was* an *easy* way down. I closed my eyes for a moment and thanked the Lord for His awesome creation.

A cutting wind sent a shiver down my spine that prompted my eyes to open. Heavy gray clouds had replaced the blue sky, and snowflakes as big as my goggles were blanketing me. I was locked into two slick pieces of wood and standing on the edge of a steep mountain surrounded by swirling snow and could see no more than five feet in front of me.

Shelley, our guide, had grown up on the slopes. She told our huddled group we were experiencing a "whiteout"—a blizzard condition that obliterates perspective and vision. She assured us that she knew this mountain like the back of her hand. She instructed us to form a single-file line, to keep our eyes focused only on the person in front of us, and to keep up the speed.

I swallowed the lump in my throat as I joined that single file. I began to ski, slowly and cautiously, as the snow got heavier. I was scared to death but had no choice but to follow the red coat in front of me if I was going to make it down this mountain.

Eventually, with my focus fixed, I lost all thought of what was around me. My fears dissipated, and I found a freedom I had never before experienced on a pair of skis. My only responsibility was to follow! I was soaring down that mountain—and I was having the time of my life!

I loosened my goggles and tugged the boots off my wobbling legs as we entered the crowded lodge. Shelley hugged me and congratulated me on skiing my first "black" slope. She explained that when the weather conditions deteriorated, she ditched the idea of taking the easy way and led us down the way with which she was most familiar—the expert-level black slope.

In less time than it took for the weather to change, my mind shifted to the spiritual. By nature, I am so cautious—so safe. I tend to opt for the easy way, the safe route. I hear the voice of the Lord, but sometimes before I take a step, I want to know what's before me, beside me, and behind me. I want to know how long it's going to take, how steep the slope will be, and how fast I'll have to go. I want to know the risks involved, how people will respond, and if the results will be positive. I want to play it safe.

Everything that would have distracted me that day—the height, the steepness, even the beauty—was obliterated by the whiteout. My only choice was to follow—and keep following. My only responsibility was to keep my eyes fixed on the leader.

The truth was evident for my life and ministry: *He* knows this "mountain" like the back of *His* hand. *He* knows the best way through the storm. And *He* will lead me all the way. When He speaks—whether I'm on a mountain or in a valley, whether I'm in my classroom or in my living room, in the daily routine or in a special ministry, whether I'm with "people of the world" or "people of the church," my only responsibility is to *fix my eyes on Jesus*—the Author and Finisher of my faith.

As a believer, my only real choice is to follow. And when I do, I experience a freedom that enables me to soar through this journey on wings like eagles.

Prayer: *Lord, when I hear you speak, when I sense your leading, help me to trust you enough to follow you—even when I can't see.*

Thought for the Day: The trail Jesus blazes for us always leads us home.

18 CALLED BY MARRIAGE? CALLED BY GOD?

patty hambrick

*I am leaving you with a gift—peace of mind and heart!
And the peace I give isn't fragile like the peace
the world gives. So don't be troubled or afraid.*
—John 14:27, TLB

In the last three weeks, sometimes with my husband, Ted, and sometimes without, I have counseled a couple in a broken marriage, encouraged a student who was about to drop out of school, attended numerous committee meetings, taught Sunday School, worked in the nursery at church, supervised and organized Children's Day, took my turn cleaning the church building, visited the sick, counseled a young pregnant woman considering abortion, comforted two mothers who lost custody of their children, sang in the choir and worship team, and helped with children's music, confronted a drug-using mother, counseled two families with children in jail, talked to my family about my father's failing health, and worked my full-time job.

This is life as a ministry wife.

Sure, I get tired. This life is rewarding, but it's hard. Demands on my time and commitment to what I must do and would like to do are difficult. But I've made a decision that blesses my soul. I believe I'm "called by God and called by marriage."

This is the 20-year anniversary of full-time ministry for Ted and me. When we got married, I didn't know he was called to ministry. In fact, when he told me I didn't believe him. I thought he was having one of those crisis experiences where you say, *God, get me out of this and I'll do anything, even preach.* When I finally realized he truly was called, I knew that God had called me too. Today I rejoice in our wonderful, challenging, exciting, difficult, adventurous, scary, and precious ministry.

Almost every time we have a difficult day, it involves miscommunication or misunderstandings in relationships within the church. In the midst of our most difficult time in ministry, Ted called one Wednesday evening and said, "I'm not going to church tonight. I'm not sure I'm ever going back." He told me what had just happened, and I had no idea how God was going to work it out. We were hurting, in deep pain, and needed a miracle.

Just then a call came that an unwed mother in our church had given birth to her baby. We were so proud of the way our people had loved this young girl back into the church and back to the Lord.

Since we weren't leading any of the numerous events that night, we went to the church dinner planning to skip church. We tried to pull ourselves together so we could go to the hospital to see the new baby and also visit a woman who was dying.

We visited the young mother on the third floor. The room was packed with many other Wednesday-night church-skippers. As we celebrated that new life, Ted picked up the baby and prayed. As he prayed, I must confess that I peeked at the sweet baby and looked around. There wasn't a dry eye. Afterward the girl's father gestured proudly around the room and said, "This is my church family." We took pictures with our digital camera, hugged everyone, and headed to the second floor.

As we visited the dying woman, it seemed that every breath would be her last. We were praying with her just as her family came through the door, and we spoke words of comfort to them. As we were leaving, they asked about our camera. Ted showed them the pictures of our new church baby. The dying woman's daughter said, "I guess there *is* something good happening, Pastor."

When we got into our car Ted said, "Patty, God just did something special for me through that young mother and the dying woman. He knew how I was hurting. It was just as though He said, 'Ted, your calling is somewhere between the second and third floors; new life and death. Good things are happening in your ministry. Be encouraged!'" That was a real turning point.

Things didn't straighten out immediately, but God used those hospital scenes to remind us that our ministry was effective, He was in charge, and He would continue to see us through.

The next day Ted got up and went to the church, and I got up and went to work. We counseled with another couple in a broken marriage; he met with a man whose wife wanted a divorce, and . . .

Prayer: *Father, give us the wisdom to stay focused on you.*

Thought for the Day: Regardless of what happens in church or life, God will take care of us when we know Him, serve Him, and obey His call.

19

MADE FOR MINISTRY

debbie henry

Being confident of this, that he who began a good work in you
will carry it on to completion until the day of Christ Jesus.
—Phil. 1:6

I love Phil. 1:6. It's my life verse! I see it as God's promise that He's at work in my life and will bring His plan to completion.

To be honest, I never really felt called or had any desire to be a minister's wife. When I met my future husband, John, in college, I knew he had God's call on his life. So when we got married, I knew we were headed into the ministry. However, I viewed pastoring as John's calling. I was completely dedicated to helping him, but I never stopped to grasp the fact that God had called *me* as well.

As we prepared to take our first assignment, I began to worry and fret because I had no idea what this meant for me. I was barely cognizant of my own identity at that age, much less able to grasp God's purpose and plan for my life. Frankly, I struggled silently with these feelings for many years.

My real passion, besides serving the Lord, was to be a

good wife and mom. Although I did want God to use me, I wasn't sure how to differentiate between serving Him and fulfilling a role. Being a pastor's wife seemed to entail much more than I felt I was able or willing to give. After all, ministry was John's calling, not mine.

Although I was active in numerous areas of church life, I always had the nagging feeling that what I did was never enough. Somehow I felt I didn't measure up. I thought I should be capable of so much more. I desperately *wanted* to have all the right qualifications.

The years went along as I functioned as a dutiful, supportive pastor's wife. Only John really knew about my inner uncertainties. Our parishioners always loved and accepted me, and I loved them dearly as well. I began to feel comfortable, finally settling into the rhythm of ministry life. Maybe I would be OK at this pastor's wife thing after all!

But my fears returned full scale when John informed me about our call to pastor in Kansas. The church was huge—as big as all the churches I had ever attended *combined*! The assignment was perfect for John, was made for him, but I was terrified! I just wasn't senior-pastor's-wife-of-a-megachurch material. I could never fill those shoes.

Looking back at the fears that consumed me during that transitional time, I can see how God carried me. He brought me through utter despair and a very real depression in order to get me to the place at which I could comprehend *His* truth concerning my calling and purpose. I finally embraced His assurance that His strength was made perfect in my weakness.

During my time of searching, I came to know, love, and depend on God as never before. As I studied God's Word every day, a clearer picture of His call on my life emerged. To my amazement, it was not very different from my life ambitions— to be a good wife and mother and to serve Him. God supplied me with strength, assurance, and wisdom that I had never experienced previously.

Through my quiet times with God, He gently showed me that I had been more consumed with trying to fulfill *people's* expectations rather than focusing on *His* purpose. It was incredibly liberating to realize after 20 years of ministry that if God had called me, then He considered me capable of fulfilling that call. For the first time I could finally relax and enjoy being a pastor's wife.

Too many times we pastor's wives feel guilty for not fitting into a certain pattern. When God created us, He didn't make molds so we would all be the same. He's far more creative than that! He designed each of us with individual gifts and talents to use for Him.

So I learned that when we quit exhausting ourselves by trying to fulfill a *position*, we can relax into His plan for us. Then He will complete His work in and through us, because our Heavenly Father always keeps His promises. And He finishes everything He begins.

Prayer: *Thank you, Father, for designing, using, and uniquely creating us to bring glory to you.*

Thought for the Day: God's design is divine.

20 HOW MUCH CAN YOU AFFORD?

mary alice hoover

Then the king was filled with pity for him, and he released him
and forgave his debt. But when the man left the king,
he went to a fellow servant who owed him a few thousand dollars.
He grabbed him by the throat and demanded instant payment.
(Matt. 18:27-28, NLT)

My husband, Mark, preached awesome messages at both services that Sunday morning. The presence of the Holy Spirit was real, and many responded to the invitation. We were rejoicing.

After church we decided to go out for lunch. Just as we were going into a local restaurant, a couple we knew was coming out. Those dear people were among a small group that had criticized our ministry very severely and then left our church in protest a few years earlier.

As our young son and I went into the restaurant to get our names on the waiting list, Mark went out of his way to greet them. He asked, "How are you doing?"

The man replied gruffly, "About the same." Then the man asked with a little smirk, "How are things going for *you*?"

It would have been easy for Mark to tell him about the momentous services crammed with people and that there were a record number of visitors in attendance and that many decisions had been made. Instead, he responded graciously, "Things are going just fine."

When we finally sat down to order our meals, Mark told me what had happened. Then he went on to explain his gentle response. He said, "I felt so sorry for him in his misery. I didn't have the heart to tell him just how wonderful the day had been."

He went on to say, "God has been so good to us that I could afford to be gracious to him." After all, what would have been accomplished if Mark had chosen to respond in kind? If he had gone on and on about the blessings that were being poured out upon our congregation, it would have just irritated our former member to an even greater extent, like rubbing salt into an open wound.

We read in Prov. 15:1, "A gentle answer turns away wrath, but a harsh word stirs up anger." Through the years we have experienced many hurtful situations. Every time we've chosen a gentle response, God has honored it. After all, our Lord told us in Matt. 5:38-39, "You have heard that it was said, 'Eye for eye, and tooth for tooth.' But I tell you, Do not resist an evil person. If someone strikes you on the right cheek, turn to him the other also."

Mark's response made me think of the unforgiving servant Jesus told about. He had been forgiven so much that he should have certainly felt the wealth of that grace. Instead, he set out to demand payment from his coworker as if he were still bankrupt.

As ministry wives, we'll be tempted to demand justice from those who hurt us. There will always be occasions when people will attempt to do damage to us personally, to our family members, or to our ministry. It's particularly difficult when the painful encounters involve family. The natural response is to register the hurts and hold onto them. Or even worse, we'll be tempted to take things into our own hands and confront the person who has hurt us.

I love what Jesus goes on to tell us in Matt. 5:43-44: "You have heard that it was said, 'Love your neighbor and hate your enemy.' But I tell you: Love your enemies and pray for those who persecute you." That's about as straightforward as it can be.

Before we set out to demand justice, we need to reevaluate all that's been extended to us. How much grace can I afford to extend? Because of the extravagant grace and mercy I've been given, I'm so deeply indebted that there's no way I can afford to be anything but gracious in return.

Prayer: *Thank you, Lord, for pouring your mercy and grace over us. Give us the grace to always respond with loving kindness and tender mercy.*

Thought for the Day: "Give, and it will be given to you. A good measure, pressed down, shaken together and running over, will be poured into your lap. For with the measure you use, it will be measured to you" (Luke 6:38).

RIDING THROUGH THE RAINBOWS

joyce williams

I have set my rainbow in the clouds.
—Gen. 9:13

It started out as a somewhat normal day in my home-town of Roanoke, Virginia. My husband, Gene, and I live halfway across the country, and such visits are rare gifts to be treasured.

I met my sisters, Bobbi and Jane, for lunch at Red Lob-ster—a favorite place. We did our normal thing of catching up, laughing, and eating too many biscuits. It was fun to be together—three sisters grabbing brief moments in time.

After a long lunch, Bobbi had to leave, so Jane and I walked out with her. We stood by Jane's cute little VW bug and talked awhile. When she tried to start her car, it wouldn't even whimper.

I called road service. About an hour later an old tow truck with a long trailer pulled up. Out oozed a greasy mechanic dressed in bib overalls. It was quite obvious he hadn't used his Right Guard or seen a shower for a while.

I could tell my little sister was a tad reluctant to have him squeeze behind the wheel of her car for fear he would leave a permanent greasy souvenir! Even with his know-how, he couldn't get the motor to turn over. Finally he said, "Ma'am, your car is broke!"

Clouds had begun to gather, and we could hear distant thunder, so we called the dealership where Jane had bought the car, and they said to have it towed there. She watched anxiously as the mechanic drove off, reluctantly leaving her treasured bug in his greasy hands.

We got into my rental car and headed across town. Looking back, I know that it was a God thing that Jane's car broke down, because those rare hours were really awesome. I can't remember the last time the two of us had been together like that with no real agenda and no hurry to be anywhere. My visits between ministry assignments always seem too packed with things to do. But that day God did some special things.

Right after we got into my car, rain poured down. Thunder rumbled while lightning flashed around us. Once we even had to pull over because we couldn't see where we were going.

But the most awesome thing of all was the parade of rainbows that began slicing through the rain. What a magnificent show! It was as though we were riding through the rainbows—one right after the other. The multihued colors seem to be painted across our faces! It was fantastic. If the legendary pot of gold had been for real, we would have found it!

I was especially touched that day because the rainbow is a sign that God's promises will be fulfilled. Tears filled my eyes as I recalled that after the deluge ended and the waters receded, God promised Noah, "I have set my rainbow in the clouds, and it will be the sign of the covenant between me and the earth. Whenever I bring clouds over the earth and the rainbow appears in the clouds, I will remember my covenant between me and you and all living creatures" (Gen. 9:13-15).

Hope—that's what rainbows are all about! God has promised to take care of us regardless of how far we roam. Our ministry to pastors and their families, known as Shepherds' Fold Ministries, has taken Gene and me to the ends of the earth—literally. We've visited 20 countries since "retirement" in 1998. Gene says, "If this is retirement, we're going to get jobs!" His definition for retirement is re-tiring the car with a new set of Michelins!

Many times we find ourselves thousands of miles and several time zones from home. Regardless of where we are, when we get weary or homesick, God always sends a promise—a rainbow of encouragement and renewal. Regardless of the storms that come into our lives, He always provides an umbrella of hope splashed across the clouds.

Sharing that precious kaleidoscope of rainbows with Jane is a priceless jewel I have tucked carefully into my treasure box of memories. I'll carry it with me as long as I live.

And when the next storm comes, I'll pull out that memory—and anticipate the rainbows.

Prayer: *Thank you, Father, for precious, treasured rainbows of memories shared with those we love.*

Thought for the Day: Jesus holds the key to the treasure house of our Father's promises.

22 GOD'S FAITHFULNESS

joyce jothi

I will never leave you nor forsake you.
—Heb. 13:5, NKJV

Fear raced with us as we rushed to the hospital early that morning. Jason, our second son, was just 10 days old. From the day he was born, he had choked every time I nursed him, suffering from blockages that prevented him from keeping his food down. So our days and nights had been filled with anxiety and tears.

As we hurried along, I remembered a special promise God had given me during other crises. I kept repeating those words: "I will never leave you nor forsake you" (Heb. 13:5, NKJV). I knew the Holy Spirit was surrounding us as we rushed down the road.

Jason was underweight at birth. He had not gained weight because of his frequent choking. As a matter of fact, he had lost some weight. We were extremely concerned about him. When we got to the hospital, the doctor refused to treat him since it was so late at night.

The receptionist told us that we would have to take Jason

to another hospital. We fought tears as we dashed between clinics and hospitals. Nobody would accept our sick little boy.

Terrified we would lose our precious baby, my husband, Simon, and I prayed together right there in the street: *Lord, you are our only help.* As soon as we prayed those few words Jason woke up and sneezed. Immediately the blockages were cleared! We rejoiced all the way home because he was out of danger without any medical help. We knew that the Lord had intervened and touched our Jason.

We still had concerns about our son. The doctor gave us medications that helped him, and we continued to pray for him to develop normally. Over the next few months he slowly gained weight. It was quite a challenge to keep up with our very intense ministry assignments as we cared for Jason and his big brother, Solomon.

We finally began to recover somewhat from that night as Jason's choking began to stabilize. Then late one evening in our kitchen, he fell from a height of about four feet. He immediately lost consciousness, and his eyes rolled to one side. I was terrified—especially when his body began to cool.

Frantically, I called Simon, and he rushed from church. Once again, we raced to the hospital. Doctors examined Jason. They said he needed some tests and that he would have to stay in the hospital for observation to determine how the fall might affect him.

We sat in that tiny cubicle with Jason, waiting anxiously as we clenched our hands and implored the Lord to touch him once again. As Simon and I prayed and agonized, not knowing what the future held for our precious little boy, we reminded each other how just a few months earlier the Lord had most definitely spared Jason's life. It was clear that He had a special purpose for our son. So we began to be comforted once again that our Heavenly Father would see Jason safely through the present crisis as well.

As we were going through all kinds of emotions, Jason suddenly roused and started to play. It was obvious that he had turned a corner. The doctor came in and said that he was out of danger. We praised God and thanked Him for His faithfulness in once again restoring Jason to us.

Sometimes those of us who are ministry wives may feel overwhelmed with our ministry responsibilities along with our parenting responsibilities. But every day I take time to praise God for His great love and goodness toward us. We can share from our hearts that His love and faithfulness will keep us through every situation that may come into our lives.

Jason is now three years old. He's a healthy, very active toddler. We know that God inspired us to give him the right name. Jason means *healing*.

Our son is truly living out the meaning of his name.

Prayer: *Thank you, our Great Physician, for your healing touch.*

Thought for the Day: Tough situations teach us to trust God in ways that peaceful times cannot.

23 PAIN PASSES. BEAUTY REMAINS

debbie keener

These have come so that your faith—
of greater worth than gold ... may be proved genuine.
—I Pet. 1:7

One rainy day I stood outside my daughter's junior high school anticipating the stampede. The bell rang. The first student through the doors looked at the rain, slumped his shoulders, and shuffled off, mumbling a bunch of words that aren't in Webster's dictionary. Amazingly, the very next guy looked at the same rain and came to life. He threw open his arms, tipped his head back, and attempted to catch the raindrops! I giggled as he bounced away! And I thought, *Isn't it interesting that two people who experienced exactly the same circumstance could respond so differently?*

The rain falls on everyone. (See Matt. 5:45.) No one is exempt, not even those of us in ministry. Some of us are blessed and have to deal only with an annoying sprinkle or a passing shower. Others of us, however, get pounded by a devastating hurricane that leaves us wondering which way is up. Funny thing—the intensity of the storm is not what determines how you weather it!

Chris was a young wife and mother of three in our church whom everyone loved. She was a magnetic and joyful believer, and she recently fought a losing battle with cancer. After Chris died, my friend Janice picked up her (Janice's) mail one day and noticed an envelope with Chris's return address. She quickly opened it and discovered something that she'll always treasure—a handwritten note from Chris telling her how special she is. In Chris's final hours, she focused on blessing others rather than dwelling on her own pain.

Pain is a reality. Life is messy. Ministry is challenging. Very few of us get to walk on a smooth road through life. Most are forced to take the rugged mountain pass that looks impossible. Even worse is the lonesome valley that seems so deep we wonder if we'll ever get out of it. So how can we be the kid who throws his arms out and catches the raindrops? How can we be the person who smiles in the midst of her pain? How can we be like Chris, who in her last days focused on being a blessing?

It's a secret far greater than seeing the glass as half full. It requires a deep confidence that "our light and momentary troubles are achieving for us an eternal glory that far outweighs them all" (2 Cor. 4:17). In order to survive and even thrive in the midst of pain, we must keep an eternal perspective.

That's what Jesus did when He endured the Cross. He paid a temporary price for an eternal prize. He knew His suffering had purpose, and He kept the end in mind.

I'm convinced there's no greater privilege than serving in ministry. But I've been a pastor's wife long enough to know that with the blessing of ministry comes the gift of pain. I will be hurt. I won't be able to live up to the expectations. I will be judged. I will be misunderstood. And unless I remember why I'm in ministry, this reality could leave me running for the closest door.

When we live with an eternal perspective, however, our pain becomes a gift. Our determination to finish well is strengthened because we perceive that our present pain is small compared to the joy we'll experience for eternity. Pain actually provides an opportunity to become more like Jesus. And when that happens, our pain becomes more precious to us than gold, because we realize that gold perishes, while faith remains.

The great painter Renoir suffered with a debilitating form of arthritis. In the last decade of his life, he was in so much pain he couldn't leave his house. Yet every day, he got out of bed and struggled to the canvas to paint.

After watching this daily battle, his close friend finally couldn't stand it anymore. He looked at Renoir and blurted out, "Why in the world, when you're in so much pain, do you continue to paint?"

Renoir gave this beautiful response: "The pain passes, but the beauty remains."

Prayer: *Dear Jesus, you reminded us that in this world we will have trouble. Please comfort our hurting hearts. Bring a reassuring confidence that it will all be worth it when we join you in heaven.*

Thought for the Day: Allow the pain to serve its purpose, and the world will be awed by Christ's beauty in you.

24

CRISIS PEACE
linda lewis

When I am afraid, I will trust in you.
—Ps. 56:3

It was a day our family had looked forward to—the arrival of our second grandchild. Our son, Andy, and his wonderful wife, Paula, had already blessed our lives with precious, red-haired Hannah. We could hardly wait to see if this little boy also had red hair, as that was not common in either family.

Andy had joined the Coast Guard Reserves after 9-11 and was stationed in Guantanamo Bay, Cuba. He had made arrangements to come home two weeks before Paula's due date. Her parents were coming. Everything was perfectly planned for a joyous two-family adventure sharing this precious baby's arrival.

The baby, of course, had his own set of plans—to arrive three weeks early instead of two. Paula and Hannah were staying with us during Andy's absence. So Paula awoke our daughter, Angela, early one morning with the news that she was in labor! We got Paula to the hospital and stayed by her side all day. When it was obvious that labor was intensifying and birth was imminent, my husband, Ernie, brought Hannah to the family waiting room across the hall from Paula's birthing room.

The doctor and nurses came in to set up the necessary equipment for the baby's delivery. When all this busyness slowed, I realized I had gotten stuck behind the delivery tray at the foot of the bed, so I had a clear view of the emerging baby.

Paula did all the hard work necessary to deliver him. After the head emerged, we waited excitedly to see the rest of the baby. But it didn't happen—and it didn't happen. His shoulders were too broad! The doctor and nurse worked feverishly to reposition the baby several times to help the shoulders slip through.

Suddenly, a distress call was shouted down the corridor. "Nurse! Triage! Nurse! Triage!" An army of nurses came running down the hall, descending on Paula's room. Poor Ernie, across the hall with Hannah, saw the commotion and knew there was trouble. There was nothing he could do. He prayed.

The doctor and nurses continued various methods of pushing, pulling, and repositioning. I was overwhelmed with fear. I couldn't watch any longer. With indescribable desperation and helplessness, I found a chair and cried out to God for help and mercy.

As I continued to pray, the Bible verse I had just shared with my children in the Christian school where I taught came to my mind. "When I am afraid, I will trust in you" (Ps. 56:3). I have trusted God since I was a child, and I knew I could trust Him with this crisis.

Immediately I calmed down as peace swept over my mind and soul. *God knows all about this situation, and He cares, He loves us, He loves this little baby.* I stood up and rejoined the crisis just in time to see my grandson, Andrew Ernest, born into this world. I felt the great relief shared with everyone else in what had been one tense birthing room!

However, that relief was short-lived as we quickly realized the baby was not breathing, not making a sound, not moving. The doctor handed little Andrew to the nursing team. After what seemed like an eternity—probably about five minutes—we heard the first, blessed soft baby sound. After letting Paula see her baby, the nurses quickly took Andrew to the infant ICU for intervention and observation. "When I am afraid, I will trust in God" became my theme song. Andrew Ernest is now a healthy, incredibly energetic three-year-old with beautiful red hair.

His birth was not the only miracle that day. Andy had been raised in a parsonage and knew about living for the Lord. But he had chosen a different course.

We talked by cell phone several times throughout the crisis. I told him to pray as never before. Andy told us later that he went to his room and finally acknowledged that in his spiritual state he couldn't even pray for his wife and baby. At that moment he asked God to forgive him, and he rededicated his life to the Lord.

I praise God for peace during times of crisis.

Prayer: *Thank you, Father, for answering a mother's prayers.*

Thought for the Day: God still works in mysterious ways to perform His wonders.

25

COMING TO HIM

gail macdonald

Come to me, all you who are weary and burdened,
and I will give you rest.
—Matt. 11:28

It has become painfully clear to me during the past decade that the number of discontented women in ministry is mounting. Why is this? I wonder if we've bought into the idea taught by our culture that satisfaction in life amounts to how much stuff we own and how much control we have.

My husband, Gordon, and I are attempting to downsize—to relinquish "stuff" and control. This has caused us to think about *intentionally* pursuing contentment. In short, discontent in my journey has become a red flag. I remind myself that Paul warned Timothy to "watch your life . . . closely" (1 Tim. 4:16).

Are we aware that advertisements can plant seeds of discontent? Some tell us our minds are filtering up to 2,000 daily messages of "you need this." Ouch! Knowing the hearts of women who are committed to serving Christ, I truly believe we want to know how to overcome this. Here are some thoughts on how I'm *trying* to confront discontentment.

Ultimately, it's all about coming to Christ, as we're invited to do in Matt. 11:28. When I go to things and people for inner rest and peace rather than to Christ, I'll be discontented. The only way back is to return to the source of our joy—Jesus himself. Then we lay our discontent at His feet.

Yes, I know all the excuses—I've used them myself. But the truth is, this is *not optional*. My personal relationship with Him is more important than any other relationship. Listening to what He has to say to me demands silence—lots of it.

For example, I usually handle the fishbowl of ministry quite well. One Sunday, though, I knew I was in trouble. I felt like weeping and didn't know why. I couldn't stand the scrutiny any longer. I turned to Gordon and told him I was leaving the first service to go home to be still before the Lord.

The very act of admitting that inner chaos had taken over seemed to set the stage for the Holy Spirit to come and flood me with reasons for my confusion and discontent. I sat before my computer and let the Holy Spirit speak through my fingers.

Soon I was overwhelmed by how much had been building up that I couldn't deal with until I took the extended time of silence—things I was *pretending* I didn't know had to be acknowledged.

The list was long. The first items to surface were what others had said or done. But the loving Spirit of Christ graciously reminded me that I needed to repent of many of my own attitudes and actions. When I did, I felt washed, refreshed, renewed, and eager to return to our congregation.

One thing is certain: I must practice relinquishment of ownership each day, because it's all on loan. John the Baptist said, "A man can receive only what is given him from heaven" (John 3:27).

For years I've written that these times of silence are our inner "fire" with Christ—that place where we're intentionally warmed by His presence. Since the fire can easily be extinguished, it has to be stirred, fed, blown on. Otherwise, it will no longer warm us or anyone else. In fact, if ignored, this Christ-fire can become cold and lifeless embers.

More than 40 years ago I heard an elderly missionary say, "An untended fire soon becomes a heap of ashes." I've clung to this truth. When I feel myself becoming spiritually distant, I ask myself, *Gail, how's your fire with Christ today? Don't you think you need to come to Him?* I can't delegate this to others. If I don't take personal responsibility, it won't happen.

In every phase of ministry life, we face temptations that demand the holy presence of Christ to keep us on track. Younger women may be tempted to think they can do it all in their own strength through natural talents and gifts. Middle-aged women may find that the crush of responsibilities distracts them from silence and time "at the fire." And older adults may be tempted to exchange the inner fire disciplines for a play ethic, turning more serious spiritual growth over to the young because they've paid their dues.

Yes, it's true that women of all ages may be enticed toward a discontented mind-set. The antidote is to realize that it's all on loan to us and to daily offer everything back to Christ. Then our Christ-fire will burn brightly, warming our hearts and those around us.

Prayer: *May we come to you to enjoy quiet seasons—sitting at your feet and basking in the enveloping fire of your presence.*

Thought for the Day: There is great beauty in a woman who is content.

26 A STEP OF FAITH

edie macpherson

"I know the plans I have for you," declares the Lord, "plans to prosper you and not to harm you, plans to give you hope and a future."
—Jer. 29:11

Talk about culture shock! My husband, Corey, and I were absolutely sure God had called us to move from Kansas to plant a new church on Long Island, New York, in 2000. As a Long Island native, Corey had no problems adjusting. It was different for me—a young wife originally from Tennessee. Starting our ministry together in such a vastly different culture from my own stretched me to the limit.

During my second year as a pastor's wife on Long Island, I came to a real crisis point. We were both working full-time. Corey was bivocational. On weekends he shifted gears to prepare his message and the Sunday service. We had a new baby girl. On a good day we tag-teamed and ended up seeing each other about an hour. We were exhausted.

Trying to start a church in an affluent and diverse area with many cultures and religious beliefs was a huge challenge. In the politically correct society, proclaiming Jesus as the only way to the Father was considered offensive—even to many "Christians."

Most Long Islanders are prosperous natives with their own deeply-established families and social groups. What few needs there are seem to be met by everything *except* Jesus.

I began to understand that these people didn't need me and probably didn't care if I was there. Those feelings deepened as I continued to encounter the unfamiliar culture and outright assertiveness so different from my background.

When I shared some of those challenges with another pastor, she replied, "To live here you just have to develop a thick skin!"

I later told Corey about that remark and in frustration exclaimed, "I don't *want* to develop a thick skin!" So I withdrew. After all, if I didn't have a thick skin, why would I *want* one?

As our two-year anniversary on Long Island approached, I became even more exhausted and lonely. I began to realize rather dreadfully, *I don't like living here!* and asked myself, *What am I going to do? How long will we have to stay? What if I'm stuck here forever?*

That summer we returned to Kansas for vacation and attended our home church on Sunday. Our pastor spoke about God's promises and said they are as relevant today as when He first spoke them. I needed to hear those words.

As we got ready to leave for the airport, I told Corey, "I don't want to go back." He wasn't surprised. I asked, "Why should I return to a place where people don't care about me and don't even seem to know I'm there?"

It just didn't seem logical. Sometimes, though, logic and obedience are two different things. I was learning that God cares about obedience. I boarded the plane reluctantly, yet knowing I could rely on His promises. Deep within my heart I knew that His purpose and plans for us on Long Island were far from completed.

So in response to our pastor's message, I began seeking out and meditating on God's promises such as Jer. 29:11; Josh. 1:5; Ps. 27:1; Isa. 41:4; Hag. 2:4-5; Isa. 32:17; Gal. 6:9; 1 Thess. 5:16-17; and many more.

As I focused on the reality of these passages, I realized that my desperate attempt to guard against developing a "thick skin" was somehow creating within me a hardened heart that prevented me from loving my people and community as God wanted me to. My deep loneliness began to turn into a hunger to study the Word and to search the mind and heart of God so that I could know Him like never before. As I saturated myself in His promises, I knew I had to make a choice: to continue to withdraw or to surrender.

Long Island still doesn't feel quite like home. But I've learned to be content and to deeply love our people. I've also learned that feeling at home isn't really the issue. God has called me to invest my life here at this time. By focusing on Him, *He* becomes the issue.

And He renews me each day with His promises.

Prayer: *Thank you, Father, for always being my neighbor—regardless of where I live.*

Thought for the Day: Home is found near the Good Shepherd's heart.

27 OUR FAITHFUL GUIDE

ellen mcwhirter

*The LORD said to Abram, "Leave your country, your people
and your father's household and go to the land I will show you."*
—Gen. 12:1

There is no doubt the blessed Holy Spirit is working actively today in our world and in the lives of all who respond to Him. He is as present now in Minneapolis as He was long ago in Mesopotamia, and as present in California as in ancient Chaldea. Could anything be more comforting and fortifying for God's people? Many years ago I saw an example of this truth in the lives of my parents as they responded to the call of the Holy Spirit.

Few memories of my childhood are as indelible as a particular evening when I was five years old and was sitting with my parents and younger brother around the dinner table. Mother and Dad were kind, loving, and morally good, but they didn't go to church or know the Lord as their personal Savior.

That evening I heard them speak about spiritual things for the first time. They were experiencing a strong and undefined spiritual hunger. Amazingly, this took place without a preacher, a teacher, or a church to guide them. They were recipients of the direct, supernatural, convicting work of the Holy Spirit.

As we sat at the table that night, I listened as they talked about how to find a church. Mother had been born and raised Catholic but had never become a practicing Catholic. Dad had a generic Protestant background but very little association with any specific church.

Then Dad remembered his Cousin Hershel, who was active in a small rural church nearby. Although Dad didn't know what kind of church it was, Mother urged him to call Hershel. So Dad got up from the dinner table and made the call. He asked Hershel if he still attended church. Hershel said he did and invited our family to go with him the following Sunday. He also invited us to his home for Sunday dinner.

The most memorable and perhaps the most formative Sunday of my life dawned when our family went to church together that day. After the morning service, we went home with Cousin Hershel for lunch. We were about to leave when the family asked us to stay and go to the evening service. We did.

That night, when the invitation was given, Dad led our family down the aisle to the altar. We just stood there for a few minutes, not sure of what to do, until the minister asked us to kneel. At the altar that night my parents were born again.

Dad immediately gave up chain smoking and social drinking. He and Mother became exuberant soul-winners, leading many of our relatives and friends to Christ. Our home abruptly changed from Christ-less to Christ-centered. The flurry of radical change was astounding.

Although Abraham lived in a different time from that of the modest and obscure lives of my parents, I see a breathtaking analogy. Not altogether unlike with my mother and father, the call of God apparently went to Abraham without a prophet, a preacher, or a teacher of the true and living God to guide or instruct him.

In a flourishing and, for that time, advanced but pagan civilization, Abraham received a supernatural, direct word from God. God called him to leave his homeland, break forever with the only country and culture he had ever known, and journey toward an unknown destination.

Some 40 centuries after Abraham's day and half a world away, the same Holy Spirit who moved in the life of Abraham also moved in the lives of my parents. As with Abraham, without the guidance of a preacher, religious leader, or a church, the Holy Spirit led our family to Christ and the Church.

Had it not been for this, it's likely my own life would have taken a vastly different and non-Christian path. As the Holy Spirit guided my steps, I met and married Stuart, an international evangelist of the gospel. What a blessing it's been to share with him in ministry across North America and on five other continents!

I thank God for calling my parents and that they answered Him. And I'm so grateful that He has literally directed my footsteps to the uttermost parts of the world.

Prayer: *Thank you, blessed Holy Spirit, for your divine guidance.*

Thought for the Day: Abundant spiritual strength is found in meditation on the reality of the Holy Spirit dwelling with and in every child of God today.

WHEN LOVE IS NOT ENOUGH

joyce mehl

I have loved you with an everlasting love.
—Jer. 31:3

The Mehl family was enjoying corn on the cob and other dinner delicacies when a familiar ring intruded into our family time at the table—a noise that seemed to accompany our mealtimes so frequently.

My pastor husband, Ron, and my two young sons looked up from their corn. "Don't anybody move!" I said. "Just keep eating. I'll get it."

Reluctant to leave my little family in that moment, I got up from the table to silence the shrill ringing. The little black "creature" sitting on the desk always seemed to intrude at dinnertime—as soon as we sat down at the table to eat. I was convinced there was some invisible connection between the creature and the table!

My frustration must have come across on the phone, because the voice on the other end seemed a little apologetic as she asked to speak to the pastor. She also sounded troubled, maybe even desperate. I immediately felt ashamed of my frustration.

As I set the receiver down to get Ron, the Holy Spirit spoke into my heart. *Love is not convenient.* He only had to say those four little words to bring my mind back to something He had said to me in the early years of our pastorate.

In our small but growing church, we had a couple with very deep and demanding needs. Honestly, I had lost track of the number of middle-of-the-night phone calls and rescue missions involving this couple. It was during one of these wee-hour events that I first felt my frustration rising.

"Why can't they ever have a problem when it's convenient?" I said to Ron. "Why does it always have to be in the middle of the night?"

Immediately the words of the Holy Spirit came in the form of a question: *Do you love these people?*

Of course I do, I thought.

But I knew what He was saying to me. I loved them when it was convenient. I loved them when it didn't interfere with my sleep or my schedule. It wasn't that I didn't love them, but I loved them with *my* love, not His love.

And that just wasn't enough.

When we first responded to God's call to come to the church, I was afraid and felt inadequate in every way. I wanted to be the kind of pastor's wife who pleased Him and humbly served the people He was entrusting to us. I felt such a tremendous responsibility. But what could I do? I couldn't play the piano. I couldn't sing. I couldn't lead worship.

As I shared these feelings with a dear friend and mentor, a wise and experienced pastor's wife herself, she said something to me I've always remembered.

With a smile she said, "But, Joyce—you can love these people."

As I've thought about that smile in later years, I suspect that an unspoken comment went along with it, maybe something like this: *And you'll learn that your love is not enough—it must be His love that works through you.*

My love gets tired and gives up hope. My love gets frustrated and disappointed. In other words, my love fails. But His does not. His love mounts up on wings of eagles and does not grow weary. (See Isa. 40:31.) His love is an everlasting love. (See Jer. 31:3.) Nothing can separate us from His love—not death, life, angels, principalities, powers, things present, things to come, height, depth, nor any other creature. (See Rom. 8:38-39, KJV.)

Not even schedules, sleep, or dinner!

I have a dear little four-year-old friend, my grandson Warner. Warner loves me, and I love him passionately. When Warner was just two years old, he had a special way of saying good-bye when he left my house.

He would stretch his chubby little arms as wide as he could and exclaim, "Grandmommie, I love you more than the whole wide world!"

And I knew he meant it. I knew that Warner would do anything in the whole wide world for me—anything, that is, that a two-year-old can do!

But someone else also stretched His arms out for me—and for you, too. It was Jesus Christ.

But His arms weren't stretched out for a hug. His hands were nailed to a Roman cross. His arms stretched wide on that cross said to the whole wide world, "I love you—more than my own life, more than anything."

Can we say that to the hurting and the lonely? Are we willing to open our arms to the desperate and the sick and love them more than anything in the world?

More than our own desires?

More than our own needs?

More than our own plans?

And maybe even more than a quiet Sunday dinner and corn on the cob?

Prayer: *Dear Father, may we love with your love.*

Thought for the Day: When we allow God's love to flow *into* us, we're available for God's love to flow *through* us.

29 A VERY PRESENT HELP

annie montgomery

God is our refuge and our strength, an ever-present help in trouble.
—Ps. 46:1

It was a gloriously perfect summer day. The sun was bright, the sky was crystal clear, and the whole earth was full of God's glory! I'll never forget the date—June 19, 2003—two days before my 53rd birthday.

On that day, my sweet husband, Lincoln, had taken me to lunch at one of our favorite spots. Then he told me to meet him at the mall to pick out my birthday gift! I was excited and surprised. Afterward, we kissed good-bye. Lincoln headed back to the church we pastor, and I headed back to work.

A few moments later, as I sat at a stoplight waiting for the red light to turn green, I felt a crushing jar and heard a hissing sound—my tires spinning out of control. I had looked down at my CD player and hadn't seen what hit me.

Suddenly I felt as if I were in a whirling ride at an amusement park. Although it seemed like an eternity, it took several seconds for me to comprehend what was happening—I had been hit by another vehicle.

I cried *Jesus!* and braced myself as my car slammed into pole after pole and took down a row of hedges before finally coming to a stop. My head hit the steering wheel so hard I was stunned and shocked by the intensity of the pain.

My natural instinct was to panic, but I don't know how to describe what happened except to say that I tangibly experienced the presence of the Lord. I felt, heard, saw, smelled, and tasted Him soothing my fears and easing my anxiety. In my most vulnerable moment, I never panicked, and a sense of calm and peace overwhelmed me.

Several people stopped and came to my aid. An off-duty firefighter stayed with me and called Lincoln, who arrived within minutes. I heard the siren of the ambulance and the voices of police officers, paramedics, Lincoln, and even an old classmate. But it was the presence of the Lord that was riveting. I never panicked—I was safe in the presence of my Lord.

Paramedics strapped me onto a gurney with a brace around my neck and raced me to the nearest hospital. After administering a series of tests and examinations, the doctors said I was "lucky" to be alive and released me.

As my family gathered around me, tears ran down my face. They thought I was hurting, but they were actually tears of joy and amazement for all I had experienced in the presence of the Lord.

The next day my eyes were black and blue, my head was bruised, swollen, and painful, and my whole body ached. It was weeks before I looked normal again, and I continued to experience headaches for almost a year. The sweet little car Lincoln had given me for my 50th birthday, three years before, was crushed like an accordion by the large pick-up truck that crashed into me at full speed. It didn't matter—I had experienced God's presence.

I learned long ago that God promised never to leave us. He is a very present help in the time of trouble, and even though we may walk through the valley of the shadow of death, He's with us. I knew by faith that He had been there during many crises over the years. But somehow this time was different—or maybe I was different. I experienced the presence of the Lord.

Why? Well, I truly believe that God used my accident as a testimony to doubters that God is with us. He's real. He's our great Jehovah God.

David and Paul eloquently describe what I experienced. In Ps. 139:7 David wrote, "Where can I go from your Spirit? Where can I flee from your presence?" Paul wrote, "I am convinced that neither death nor life, neither angels nor demons, neither the present nor the future, nor any powers, neither height nor depth, nor anything else in all creation, will be able to separate us from the love of God that is in Christ Jesus our Lord" (Rom. 8:38-39).

No, I'll never forget that gloriously perfect summer day. For that was the day I experienced the incredible presence of the Lord in a powerful new way.

Prayer: *Thank you for your encompassing presence.*

Thought for the Day: Our Father holds us in times of trouble.

ROBINS DON'T HAVE WRINKLES

joyce williams

Look at the birds of the air; they do not sow or reap or store away in barns, and yet your heavenly Father feeds them. Are you not much more valuable than they?
—Matt. 6:26

Deep in thought, I scuffled through the moist, dying leaves of the Kansas woods on that morning in early winter a few years ago. Hands thrust snugly into the pockets of my hooded jacket, I trudged along, glancing up from time to time. Burdens and cares were pressing deeply on my soul, and I could almost tangibly feel the weight of the heavy load. My brow was wrinkled with anxiety.

Suddenly a flash of faded red flitted among the trees above me. As I slowed my pace, I was amazed to see a lone robin perched on a branch, chirping. What was a robin doing so far north this time of the year? And how could he sing in the frosty air? Had he misunderstood his flock's flight schedule? How had he missed the departure time set for migrating to the sultry, sunny South? Before I could stop myself, I began to worry about that robin. After all, what was one more worry in a long list?

Then my Father began to chide me. Why was I so distressed? He brought to mind His promise in Matt. 6:25-26: "I tell you, do not worry about your life. . . . Look at the birds of the air; they do not sow or reap or store away in barns, and yet your heavenly Father feeds them."

Conviction swelled within me as I plodded on, kicking the leaves. The Lord began to teach me an old lesson in that chapel framed by the boughs of barren branches. He reminded me that although I had an earthly right to be worried, there was no heavenly reason to justify my anxiety.

It was true that the past months had been crisis-filled. My mind began to replay its anxious litany as I reviewed each difficult time. Gene and I even had to laugh and talk about how much we empathized with our Old Testament friend, Brother Job, when for several days each phone call seemed to contain a new crisis. We began to feel as though we were in the middle of the "Job syndrome." We were tempted to disconnect the phone and put our cell phones away.

Again my thoughts were drawn back to Matt. 6:34—"Do not worry about tomorrow. . . . Each day has enough trouble of its own" (NASB). Isn't that the truth? Today seemed to be on trouble overload. How could I borrow from tomorrow's troubles? It was beginning to worry me that I was worried! Now that was the ultimate in being ridiculous! I really understood the distressed cry of that father who exclaimed to Jesus, "I do believe; help me overcome my unbelief!" (Mark 9:24). Talk about paradoxical statements! Yet there it was. I would surrender my burdens and then pick them back up again.

Once more the flash of red fluttered across my path, and I watched that rounded, confident, joyous robin seemingly oblivious to the danger surrounding him. He wasn't about to let winter's frozen loneliness take away his confidence in his Creator. And my heart began to lift. I remembered the words from my Bible study of Phil. 4 that morning: "Do not be anxious about anything, but in everything, by prayer and petition, with thanksgiving, present your requests to God" (v. 6). Prayers swelled from my heart as I ran through my list.

As I continued to pray, I began to feel an indescribable enveloping pillow of peace surround me. The next verse blessed my soul: "And the peace of God, which transcends all understanding, will guard your hearts and your minds in Christ Jesus" (v. 7). Confidently I picked up my pace and repeated over and over, "I can do all things through Christ who strengthens me" (v. 13, NKJV). Renewed hope and peace permeated me as I walked back to our hotel, ready to face the next crisis.

My fine feathered friend had sparked the renewal of the essence of those ancient passages. And I praised God that His promises are not just for the birds!

Prayer: *Father, please help me to always rest in your loving care. Your promises are all I need to sustain me.*

Thought for the Day: I'm so grateful for the divine anti-wrinkle prescription outlined in the promises of the Word.

31 GUARD YOUR HEART

pam morgan

Above all else, guard your heart, for it is the wellspring of life.
—Prov. 4:23

Talk about a shock! Larry, my seemingly healthy husband of 30 years, had just been told he needed emergency open-heart surgery. We suddenly found ourselves in a hospital room trying to prepare our hearts and minds for major surgery the next morning.

We were told that if Larry's problem hadn't been discovered through a routine check-up, it could have been a matter of two or three weeks before a massive heart attack would have taken his life. Through the providence of God, the tests revealed that a genetic fluke had caused the arteries around Larry's heart to collapse. Within 24 hours of his EKG, Larry was in surgery for five bypasses.

Larry and I have known each other since we were seven years old. We always thought we would end up together. In fact, at that young age, Larry told his cousin he was going to marry me someday. Being a man of his word, he kept his promise!

Waiting in the hospital that day, I wondered what this new challenge meant for our future. I was plagued with what-ifs. What if the surgery didn't go well? What if Larry died? We loved pastoring together. Would Larry be able to continue in ministry?

That evening in the darkened hospital room while Larry slept, I was wide awake. Scripture fragments popped into my head: "Some trust in chariots and horses, but we trust in the name of the LORD our God" (Ps. 20:7, NIV, adapted). I knew those words came from a chorus I had sung, but I wondered why that particular chorus kept running through my mind.

Later I felt prompted to read Ps. 20, my scripture from earlier that day. That was the passage I kept hearing throughout the night. It begins with "May the Lord answer you when you are in distress. . . . May He send you help from the sanctuary and grant you support. . . . Now I know the LORD saves his anointed" (vv. 1-2, 6). And there it was, in verse 7: "Some trust in chariots and some in horses, but we trust in the name of the LORD our God." As I read those verses, I wept. I felt that God had spoken to me intimately and personally.

I had no idea when I hurriedly read Ps. 20 early that morning that I would be facing this crisis that very day. *God* knew, though! How thankful I am that I read His Word. He prepared me for that trial by reminding me that it's important to guard my heart through unbroken fellowship with Him.

With our children and families far away, I was tempted to feel alone during those night hours. But God knew exactly what I needed. He sent "help from the sanctuary"—a wonderful group of people from our church.

I've thought a lot about hearts since that crisis in our lives. Our physical hearts are central to our well-being, because they supply blood to the rest of our bodies. So we must protect and guard them from anything that might jeopardize our physical health.

It's the same with our spiritual hearts, the center of our Christian lives. We must protect them as well. Proverbs 4:23 says, "Above all else, guard your heart, for it is the wellspring of life." We can allow God's Word to penetrate our hearts and permeate our beings. When we hold tightly to His promises and guard them well, we'll be protected against the attacks of the evil one, who wants to discourage and keep us in a state of anxiety.

I can testify that it would have been easy to throw open the door of my heart and let anxiety and stress take over during Larry's crisis. But my Heavenly Father held me steady as I put my trust in Him and His Word.

Our prayers were answered, and I rejoice that today Larry's heart is as good as new!

God knows the problems we'll face and has already made provision for us. When we walk with Him daily, He'll guard our hearts and give us peace that's beyond understanding.

I know it's true, because He did it for me!

Prayer: *Father, thank you for keeping and guarding our commitment until the day we see you.*

Thought for the Day: Above everything else in life, we must guard the condition of our spiritual hearts.

32 TOO BROKEN TO TRUST

kelly pankratz

*Trust in the LORD with all your heart and lean not
on your own understanding.*
—Prov. 3:5

When I was eight months pregnant with our second child, my best friend, Tonya, committed suicide. I wasn't prepared for the emotional fallout of the circumstances of her death.

As the pastor's wife, I wanted to be strong for the congregation and answer the questions that accompany suicide. The best I could do was bury all my emotions at the bottom of my feet and be strong for everyone else. There was no time for me to deal with the death of my best friend, a death that came by her own hand.

Not only was I about to deliver a child, but our son was a 13-month-old toddler who needed my attention. Giving everything I had to others depleted me, and there was no more of me left for myself. I needed comfort, too; I had so many questions for God about the way Tonya died that it was hard to trust Him. I found myself blaming Him for not stopping her. I didn't know where to turn. Without realizing what I was doing, I turned to food; thus began my lifelong battle with bulimia.

While at home with the kids, I consumed food knowing that I could go to the bathroom and purge and once again feel OK. What I couldn't do was purge the emotional wounds from Tonya's death and go on pretending that nothing was wrong. I began to need more and more food to experience the comfort necessary to function on a normal level. On the inside I was a whirlwind of emotions totally out of control, but on the outside I successfully put on the facade of a pastor's wife. It didn't take long, though, until the food won out and began showing its effects on my body. My weight was increasing, and my self-esteem was decreasing. I experienced enormous guilt every day because I felt I wasn't measuring up to what a Christian should be—not to mention what a pastor's wife should be.

I saw my life as an example of the battle that rages between God and Satan. Satan was working with all his might to keep me from becoming still before God and dealing with my pain. The more I withdrew from God into the busyness of the day, the more I hurt myself. All along, God called me to Him, seeking me out. By the time I became aware that leaning on my own understanding wasn't working, I felt too deeply enmeshed in my bulimia.

The amazing thing is that we serve a relentless God. He pursued me with passion, not giving up on me even when I had given up on myself and turned to food. Through the stillness of those nights while I rocked my daughter to sleep, God poured out His deep love to me.

I would love to share with you that I've been totally healed of my battle with bulimia, but I face it every day. As only He can, God has taken bulimia and used it to draw me ever so closer, opening my eyes to the realization of my need to trust totally in Him. It's through His deep love that I came to understand that the success of my life as a pastor's wife is determined by the amount of time I spend at His feet.

It's not about who I am or what I do in my own strength. And it certainly isn't about whether I wear size 4 or size 22. God loves me for who I am on the inside, and I'll strive to be who He created me to be—a worshiper of Him.

Prayer: *Father, continue to draw me to your feet. Give me an intense desire to spend more time with you and less time focused on me.*

Thought for the Day: It's not who we are, what we accomplish, or what we look like that matters. What matters most is a life spent with Jesus.

LIFE IS STILL HAPPENING

jodie pinckard

Many are the plans in a man's heart,
but it is the Lord's purpose that prevails.
—Prov. 19:21

We anticipated Mark's birth for nine months; we never anticipated his death.

On May 20, 2002, I was tutoring a student when my principal opened the door. "Jodie, may I see you in the office?"

When I arrived, she asked me to sit down. "Mark's been in an accident. They're taking him to the hospital in an ambulance."

I knew Mark was a good driver, and he was using our three-quarter-ton Suburban that day. I was not worried when I paged my husband, Phil, who is chaplain at the Medical Center of South Arkansas. Phil's pager vibrated at 2:13. When he called back, I said I would meet him outside the emergency room.

I wasn't prepared for the blood I saw on my son and the deep moans of pain I heard from him as he was taken through the hospital doors. Anxiety, bewilderment, shock, and tears covered the faces of his friends. They just kept coming—friends in band, drama, and soccer, and classmates who graduated with him the week before. As we waited outside the emergency room, Heather, Mark's sister, was driving home from college. She intended to spend the summer with her brother.

Mark had wonderful plans for life beyond high school. He wanted to be a mechanical engineer and earn a doctorate. He knew there would be changes in his life as he wrote his essay for college: "Now I must prepare myself for the years ahead, when I must act solely on my own with no guiding light from my parents but always strive to see God's light and follow it steadfastly."

At first, although he had a broken arm and collarbone, a fractured jaw, and a bruised left lung, his condition was not life-threatening. But as they settled him into the intensive care unit, something went wrong. His pupils became uneven and unresponsive. During a "stat" CT, Mark's heart stopped once and was shocked back into rhythm. He was placed on a respirator. The CT revealed a sub-epidural hematoma. An artery had ruptured between his skull and his brain.

Heather arrived at the hospital minutes before the doctor informed us of the blood flooding Mark's brain stem. Phil knelt in front of me, took my hands in his, and said, "Honey, he's gone!" Mark's distinctive personality was gone forever.

Phil paused, then asked me, "What do you think—should we donate his organs?" I said a quiet, "Yes." As the ICU nurses maintained his body for organ recovery, clusters of his friends came into his room to see him. A few hours after giving consent, we learned that three weeks earlier Mark's French class had discussed organ and tissue donation. Mark had spoken up, saying, "If anything were to happen to me, I'd want them to take anything and everything they could use, because where I'm going, I won't need them." God had confirmed through Mark himself that we had made the right decision.

I recalled one of Mark's favorite quotes, one by John Lennon: "Life is what happens while you're busy making other plans." Even though Mark died, life would still happen as people waiting for an organ or a cornea were located.

Mark's liver, kidneys, and corneas were transplanted into five different recipients. As a healthcare chaplain, Phil frequently assists grieving families as they consent to donate organs and tissues. Donations have skyrocketed since Mark's death.

We've met only one of Mark's organ recipients. Caitlin Pendzinski was four years old when she received Mark's kidney. A very special bond has formed between our families. Two years after Mark's death, when Heather was planning her wedding, she asked Caitlin to be her flower girl.

Tears of joy filled our eyes as we watched that bright-eyed six-year-old walk down the aisle carrying a basket of rose petals. Caitlin is alive and well because of Mark's kidney. No one could have guessed that this healthy youngster was fed through a feeding tube and relied on dialysis for the first four years of her life. Truly, a part of Mark was with us on Heather's wedding day embodied in Caitlin's new life.

Despite the constant heartache and deep pain caused by Mark's death, God comforts me through others when I receive a hug, a pat on the hand, or someone says, "I miss him, too." I'm able to smile as I look at Heather's wedding pictures, because Mark's life is still happening, and the Lord's purpose prevails—through Caitlin.

Prayer: *We thank you, Father that your everlasting hope comforts us in our deepest sorrow.*

Thought for the Day: Our hope is in things eternal.

34 CHOCOLATES AND TRIALS

nancy roberts

Why are you downcast, O my soul? Why so disturbed within me?
Put your hope in God, for I will yet praise him,
my Savior and my God.
—Ps. 43:5

I never even dreamed of living in Brussels, Belgium, the chocolate capital of the world! Belgium is known for its delectable chocolates made from 48-percent pure cacao beans imported from exotic places.

A mental image of friends sitting around a table with coffee and chocolate evokes a sense of luxury and ease. However, those same friends are likely to be faced with faith-shattering experiences and severe tests that stretch them farther than they believe they can endure. Such struggles also come to those of us who are in ministry.

Twenty-two years ago we moved to a church in the heartland that had a strong organization and many gifted people. We were excited about the ministry opportunities and felt led to plant ourselves there for a long and productive pastorate. We had some great years.

However, we encountered difficult issues of power, control, and heart-wrenching problems for which there were no easy answers. Many dear people served faithfully for years, but the church finally fell prey to powerful opposition and a divisive spirit. We found ourselves severed from the church we had served for almost 20 years. We were devastated.

We sought God's will and direction as we searched the Scriptures for comfort and guidance. Again and again we surrendered everything to the Lord, asking Him to lead us through this very dark period. Our family and friends were a great encouragement. We found comfort from them as we grieved the loss of what we had thought would be our life's work.

Roger enjoyed gardening, and he had planted many trees in an empty field behind our house. For years those beautiful trees provided much-needed shade and enjoyment. But one day soon after we put our house up for sale, five bulldozers appeared, barreling across that lovely field. In just a few hours the trees were destroyed to make way for a housing development.

I was crushed. It seemed like a final blow that added insult to injury. As I wept, God reminded me that those trees had been ours to enjoy for many years until just days before our move. It seemed like confirmation that our purpose had been fulfilled.

So in the knowledge that God is sovereign, that nothing catches Him by surprise, and that He's in control of our circumstances, we trusted Him to work His perfect will in our lives and those of our church people. Many were hurting as we were. We learned to relinquish bitterness or sorrow to God and pray His blessings upon the people.

Finally our call to go to Brussels was confirmed. We joyfully embraced His will for us. It was so refreshing to anticipate a new start in an international church.

As I sorted through our belongings, I opened a fragile box that held flags I had made as a child. I had long forgotten how as a 10-year-old I had colored those flags on a worn-out bed sheet, copying the designs from my old encyclopedia. The colors were still vivid after 50 years in that box.

The flags seemed to represent the dear people in Belgium whom I would soon meet. I was overcome by the discovery of these treasures, because our new calling was to minister to a church of more than 40 nationalities. Today, when I see the beautiful faces of many colors that make up our congregation in Brussels, I see the world.

Our difficult trials truly turned out to be stepping-stones to the next stage of our lives. As Jer. 29:11 promises, none of our experiences were wasted: "'I know the plans I have for you,' declares the LORD, 'plans to prosper you and not to harm you, plans to give you hope and a future.'"

Praise God for his faithfulness! He has restored our joy, and we are blessed.

Prayer: *May each of us find joy and meaning in ministry even in the midst of tests and trials as we allow you, Lord, to work out your purpose in all things.*

Thought for the Day: Don't be surprised when God sends a box of chocolates to you in the midst of difficult times. Watch for those sweet moments of encouragement. Then take time to enjoy a few chocolates along the way!

35 TRUST, ADJUST, AND OBEY

cheryl roland

Trust God from the bottom of your heart; don't try to figure every-
thing out on your own. Listen for God's voice in everything you do,
everywhere you go; He's the one who will keep you on track.
—Prov. 3:6, TM

I wasn't sure my heart would ever join me. Although the boxes were unpacked and the house was beginning to find its warmth, I continued to watch and wait for God to fill my emptiness and give me a sense of purpose.

Serving the Lord as a pastor's wife was my joy and privilege. Our moves were few and deliberate, always bathed in prayer. It was no secret—my motto was "I shall not be moved." However, God's voice was clear, and in obedience to His calling, we would trust, adjust, and obey.

This move was unique. We would no longer be pastoring a single church but would be ministering to many churches. There was an adventure ahead if only I could muster enough faith to form a mustard seed. I seemed paralyzed, without purpose or point. There were days when I lifted my hands to serve the Lord only to realize that they were filled with anger and doubt. (See I Tim. 2:8.)

On the way to school one morning, our daughter Kari pointed out a nursing home we had passed many times but I hadn't noticed. For years, nursing home ministry was one of our joys. Could God be leading us to a familiar place of service? Both our girls, then 11 and 14, liked to go along to meet, greet, sing, pray, and encourage.

However, as I sought God for His direction, He reminded me, "Who may stand in his holy place? He who has clean hands and a pure heart" (Ps. 24:3-4). *Lord*, I prayed, *cleanse me for service, "not just my feet but my hands and my head as well!"* [John 13:9].

Our hearts went out to those dear people—especially Larry. His arms were uncooperative, and his hands were twisted into pretzel-like shapes. Just 35 years old, he spent his days in a reclined wheel chair and his nights in a hospital bed at the mercy of others to care for him. No one seemed to know what had robbed him of his mobility and paralyzed his potential. Whatever the cause, Larry was a young man in an old folks' home living with friends who were more than twice his age.

Larry faithfully attended the weekly Bible study. While teaching a series on The Lord's Prayer, I stressed that our God is the all-powerful, all-knowing, and always-abiding God. I explained that God is often referred to as Jehovah our Righteousness, Jehovah our Peace, Jehovah our Healer. I was vaguely aware that the words leaped from my lips but my faith did not follow.

"Teacher, teacher," Larry interrupted. "See my arm. It's

twisted, and my hand doesn't work. Look—what's Jehovah going to do about this?" I stopped to sympathize but went on with the many promises of Jehovah our Shepherd and Jehovah our Provider. Larry persisted: "Teacher, teacher, what's Jehovah going to do about this arm and this hand? And what about this?" He threw the lightweight blanket onto the floor, and everyone turned to see his brand-new tennis shoes tied onto lifeless feet. His youthful jogging suit would never be worn for its intended purpose. "What's Jehovah going to do about this?"

I crumbled to my knees beside his chair while others shuffled over to join us. We prayed the promise that "those who hope in the LORD will renew their strength. They will soar on wings like eagles; they will run and not grow weary, they will walk and not be faint" (Isa. 40:31).

Larry's powerful question flooded my heart with renewed faith in Jehovah my Savior. I, too, was paralyzed, but in an instant my strength was renewed as I surrendered to Jehovah, the Prince of Peace. I was to trust Him and walk in obedient anticipation.

My surrender transformed the complexion of our home. It's once again a place filled with laughter as we trust, adjust, and obey the Lord. Then, regardless of the challenges we face, we wait with faith-filled anticipation to see "What's Jehovah going to do about this?"

Prayer: *Thank you, Jehovah, for your patience with us. You're always at work in our lives, renewing our strength and filling us with the joy of obedience.*

Thought for the Day: What comfort to know we can trust God to uphold us with His righteous right hand!

36 FOR YOU I WAIT ALL DAY LONG

pam runyan

Lead me in thy truth, and teach me: for thou art the God of my salvation; on thee do I wait all the day.
—**Ps. 25:4-5**, KJV

The challenges of being a youth pastor's wife, leading college ministry, directing teen choirs, and being the mom of a three-year-old and a one-year-old are not for the fainthearted. Desperate to find some time alone with God, I set my alarm early, hoping to rise before my breakfast crowd. It seemed I no sooner sat down with my Bible than I heard little feet heading my way. I persevered during the day by kneeling at the couch to pray while the children were playing. Soon I felt little hands hugging my neck and little bodies climbing over my back. As a human Jungle Gym, it was a little hard to concentrate!

What a surprise when God called us as missionaries to the jungles of Africa in the Ivory Coast! As my husband, Doug, traveled in Rwanda, God gave promises for his safety. At home God protected the children and me as well.

As I waited before Him, God gave Isa. 54:13 to me, promising to teach my children and give them peace. God's presence settled over our household. He calmed our hearts during malaria attacks, political unrest, separation from family, depression, and cultural adjustments. He gave peace and restored energy for ministry to my family and others.

I'm convinced that Jesus knows all about the unique demands of ministry and family. People clamored to be with Him. His disciples were a needy bunch who demanded His attention as well. Even His mother made Him aware of the need for wine at the marriage in Cana.

As Jesus met the physical and spiritual needs of the multitudes, family, and close friends, He must have grown weary. After all, He was human as well as God. What did He do? We read in the Bible that He went up to the mountain to pray or rose in the night and prayed. Jesus found pleasure and strength in being with His Father.

Prayer, meditation, and waiting on God are necessities for Christians who desire lives of peace and power in ministry. We give emotionally and physically to our family and to ministry, and our energy is depleted. Following Jesus' example, waiting on our Father, our souls and bodies are restored.

It isn't always easy to wait for His strength to renew us. I haven't always succeeded. Satan loves for us to be too busy, tired, and preoccupied with good things. He knows that our strength comes from a loving God who replenishes our energy as we serve Him.

When I take time to delight in the Lord and bask in His

presence, He enables me to accomplish more. I focus on Him and His ministry opportunities. It's a special time to knock on heaven's door with the needs of my husband and now three young adult children and their spouses. God brings balance into my life and theirs as I wait on Him.

Today, as a worship pastor and senior pastor's wife in Texas, I'm even more aware of how much I need to wait on the God of perfect peace to replenish my soul. I love to follow the path Jesus took to the quiet places to be with His Father. Joy and strength are mine as I delight in His presence and listen as He speaks though His Word. Waiting before God brings clarity to my ministry.

Only through quiet meditation with our Father can we become fully aware of the imparted Spirit of God within us. The Holy Spirit quiets us, giving strength to our inner life with His love and peace. Isa. 40:31 promises, "Those who wait on the LORD shall renew their strength; They shall mount up with wings like eagles, They shall run and not be weary, They shall walk and not faint" (NKJV). The strength to walk, run, and soar comes from quietly waiting before the Lord. Run into the arms of our Father, and soar with the eagles!

Prayer: *Father, in love I wait before you. Strengthen me to be the woman you desire me to be.*

Thought for the Day: As we wait before Him today, may our Father strengthen us as He strengthened Christ. May His love, in all its fullness, be in us as we faithfully serve Him.

VICTIM OR VICTOR

gayla ryan

Surely God is my salvation; I will trust and not be afraid.
—Isa. 12:2

It was a muggy Wednesday afternoon as we neared Biloxi, Mississippi. My husband, Larry, and I were headed to the Gulf region to meet with a friend who directs a compassionate ministries organization. We wanted to determine how we could assist those who had lost their homes and possessions in the aftermath of Hurricane Katrina. Just five weeks earlier, that vicious storm had made landfall, claiming lives and leaving a path of massive destruction.

There had been no way to prepare for such enormous devastation. We rode slowly through the scenes of destruction. In our many years of ministry, I had experienced some difficult situations. Nothing compared to what we were seeing.

Larry and I were filled with shock and disbelief. How had anyone survived? How could these people ever recover? Where would they begin to pick up the pieces? What about the children? Where did so much debris come from?

Finally we met our friend at a high school football stadium. On the field was a large red-and-white tent. Generators hummed in the background.

He led us to his pickup truck. As he navigated around the mounds of rubble, he told us about that fateful night, August 29, 2005. In this area wave surges had reached 8 to 35 feet. Huge trees lay uprooted. Houses had floated off their foundations into the middle of the street. Cars were piled in great heaps and mangled into mere pieces of metal. Buildings had collapsed under the force of the wind and water.

As we continued through town, we talked to the people and heard stories of lives lost, survival, and miracles. My heart was heavy, and my emotions were torn. All kinds of questions raced through my mind.

A new friend shared this story that changed my life:

Three weeks after the hurricane, on an unbelievably hot afternoon, a crowd of more than 700 gathered in the football stadium. They were awaiting the arrival of a relief agency that would be distributing aid.

The heat intensified, but the trucks didn't come. The people became restless. After standing there for several hours, word came that the trucks weren't coming. The people would have to return another day. Tempers flared, and emotions were raw.

Slowly, nearly 500 moved toward the tent to get some shade and retreat from the heat. They were angry, grumbling and complaining.

Suddenly, out of that crowd a godly woman stood to

her feet and loudly declared, "We ought to be ashamed of ourselves. Here we are griping and complaining. We're alive! We're God's living proof that He was with us in the storm! We should be thanking God instead of griping! What the wind did we can't change, but God proved He's able to keep us even in the midst of the wind."

As that woman spoke, something began to happen. People everywhere began falling to their knees. For three hours a spirit of prayer, worship, and thanksgiving prevailed. Victims became victors.

As I thought about that woman who chose to be a victor, my mind went back to two weeks earlier when I had gone through a tough time. (It suddenly seemed very minor compared to what I was experiencing in Mississippi.) Larry left that morning just as our hot water tank quit. The roof in our two-year-old house began to leak. We had just moved and had not sold our other house. I was alone and wanted everything fixed. So I was whining to the Lord and feeling sorry for myself. Finally I said, "Lord, I don't like my attitude. Why is this happening to me? Please help me."

I opened my Bible to Isa. 12 and began to read, "God is my salvation. . . . The LORD is my strength. . . . Give thanks to the LORD. . . . Sing to the LORD." I began weeping as the Holy Spirit spoke to me. I felt so ashamed. I asked for forgiveness and started praying and praising Him. I declared, "I will not let circumstances rob me of my joy."

At that very moment I determined that I would be a *victor* over the circumstances instead of a *victim under* the circumstances. The problems were still there, but I could trust God and not be afraid.

Just like that godly lady in Biloxi, Mississippi, I had learned that praise is the first step toward victory.

Prayer: *Thank you, Lord, for caring for me.*

Thought for the Day: We can be victors in the midst of our trials.

38 ANGEL AND BLESSING FROM THE JUNGLE

joyce williams

Do not forget to entertain strangers, for by so doing some people have entertained angels without knowing it.
—Heb. 13:2

My husband, Gene, and I were deeply moved by the dear pastors and wives who gathered for the retreat near Banga- lore, India. Sharing with ministry couples is one of our favorite things as we work with Shepherds' Fold Ministries, which the Lord enabled us to establish when we "retired."

Although we were on the other side of the globe, it was amazing to us that so many needs are the same regardless of the diverse cultures and environment. Within a few minutes we felt that we had known these people for a long time.

One of the great blessings of Shepherds' Fold Ministries is that we're always being surprised with such special experi- ences. During the course of the retreat that day, a beautiful 15- year-old girl named Blessing performed a sacred dance about creation. It was very touching to see the joy splashed across her face as the ancient story was so vividly portrayed.

During the next break I went to her parents and began to talk with them. My heart was deeply moved as their story unfolded.

They were from a jungle tribe near Hyderabad. I felt humbled when they told me they had traveled for more than 20 hours by train and bus to be with us.

I asked Pastor Krishnalal how he had come to know Jesus. He said, "When I was just a little boy, a missionary lady came to our village. She told me about Jesus, and I knelt there in the dirt and asked Jesus to come into my heart. And He did! I have served Him since that day."

Then I asked his beautiful wife, Angel, how she had come to know the Lord. She said, "As a young girl, I was trained to be a sensuous dancer in the Hindu temple. I didn't know any other way to live. Then I met Krishnalal, and he told me about Jesus. It wasn't long before I had given my heart to Him as well. After we were married I began dancing for Jesus."

Tears filled my eyes as their story unfolded. Although their tribal group does not have a written language, both of them had completed their education and graduated from college. They're now pastoring and overseeing a number of churches scattered throughout the jungle with more than 1,000 believers.

I asked about Blessing, their beautiful and gifted daughter. Angel told me Blessing had been orphaned and that no one seemed to want her. She, too, was a young temple dancer. When they heard about Blessing's plight, they took her into their home and adopted her. Their only stipulation was that she would dance for Jesus rather than in the temple. It wasn't long before little Blessing gave her heart to Jesus as well.

Then three years ago the Lord blessed them further when their son was born. They named him John Wesley. It was deeply moving to see the love portrayed in this beautiful family whose glowing faces radiate the love of Jesus.

As so frequently happens on these "mission" trips, we were the ones whose hearts were deeply touch and warmed by the dear ones we encountered. I felt that I needed to sit at their feet and listen to their words of wisdom. Their vast repertoire of life experiences would make my stories pale in comparison.

That evening we reluctantly and tearfully said good-bye to that precious family as they left to begin their long trek back to the jungle. On our way back to our hotel I told Gene, "I feel like we've spent time with some of God's special ambassadors. Isn't it awesome that that sweet pastor's wife is named Angel? And how appropriate that their daughter's name is Blessing!" Our lives had truly been enriched by our new friends.

Prayer: *Father, may we always be conscious that you are constantly intersecting our lives with your special emissaries. Help us grasp each encounter from a heavenly perspective.*

Thought for the Day: Far more than we realize, angels and blessings are part of the "benefits package" our Father gives to us each day of our lives. May we embrace each moment and divine appointment as opportunities to share His love.

39

ORDINARY OR SACRED?

cindy schmelzenbach

Whatever you do, whether in word or deed, do it all in the name of the Lord Jesus, giving thanks to God the Father through him.
—Col. 3:17

It was still dark when the Fijian pastor's wife ushered in the new day, singing hymns and praying as she lit the kerosene lantern. The sounds of her worship gently awakened those of us who shared her humble thatch home that weekend. It was Sunday morning, and we were planning to go up the coast where my husband, Harmon, would be preaching in an area where the JESUS film team had been working.

Seated together in a circle on the woven mat that covered the floor, we joined her—singing songs, reading scripture, and praying together. Then we shared a cup of hot Fijian tea made with plenty of sugar and milk. She spoke in a whisper as she instructed us, "We must hurry. As soon as there's enough light to see the footpath down the mountainside, we'll leave. The tide is going out."

The unspoken implication of her simple instruction was

that every foot the tide went down meant walking what seemed like hundreds of yards farther across the shallows in order to get out to the boat. The problem was that those extra hundreds of yards were through the black sticky mud of the mangrove swamps.

The term *kidrakidra* is a Fijian word that has no direct English translation. It literally refers to the oozing-slurping sound resulting from pulling your foot out of wet, sticky mud. I've seen children sink up to their hips in mangrove mud. It is without doubt an experience worth avoiding, so I was eager to get down the mountainside as early as possible.

As we stepped into the clearing at the bottom of the hill, I looked out across the mud flats. Even in the grayness of the early-morning light, I could tell that the tide was already very low, and the boat was very far away. We took off our shoes and lifted our clothes as we stepped down into the nastiest, squishiest, stickiest mud I've ever seen. We started making that *kidrakidra* sound as we made our way out to the water's edge.

The pastor's wife had gone ahead of us and was busily washing the boat. When we got there, I looked at the spotless, dry seats we would have to step on in order to get into the boat. Then I looked at our feet, pitch-black with lumpy clay-like mud up to our knees. The last thing I wanted to do was climb in without at least trying to wash off some of the mess. While balanced on the mangrove roots, I found the risk of falling onto my face in the mud more and more likely.

She and the pastor urged us, "Just get in—don't worry about the mud!" There wasn't much choice, so we stepped over the side of the boat, onto the seats, and then down onto the white deck—filthy, muddy feet and all.

As I looked down at the mess we had made and realized that now we didn't even have a clean place to sit, I watched as the pastor's wife dipped her bucket into the seawater. She sang softly as she washed the seats a second time, cleaning them completely, and dried them.

She then turned to where we were standing, smiled brightly, and knelt down. She started washing our legs and feet, singing until every bit of the tarry mud was gone. Then, using nothing more than a ragged piece of cloth, she cleaned and dried the boat. She straightened her back and smiled again, motioning for us to sit.

Within seconds, the boat was headed out into the open ocean. As we moved over the waters, I thanked God for this precious Fijian pastor's wife. What a beautiful reminder that so much of what God calls us to do is not flamboyant but is actually very ordinary—just doing what needs to be done! My feet were really dirty, and she had washed them for me.

Jesus encountered some dirty feet one day, and He washed them. In so doing, He transformed forever that mundane task into a sacred act of worship.

Prayer: *Father, please bring into every task of every day that sanctifying perspective that transforms even the most routine activity into joyful worship—holy and pleasing in your sight.*

Thought for the Day: May the delight of worship be discovered in the ordinariness of today.

40

PERFECT PEACE

Laisa Siakimotu

You will keep in perfect peace him
whose mind is steadfast, because he trusts in you.
—Isa. 26:3

"What's wrong with Jaimie?" asked Anne. Our sons, Deane and Ritchie, ran to meet her that hot afternoon to get the special treat she always brought. But our daughter, Jaimie, just lay quietly on the couch. It was obvious something was terribly wrong.

Jaimie was a great runner. When she came home from school that day, she was upset because she had not won a race. Running had become a struggle. We had noticed a few bruises, but since she was so active, we thought she had been bumping into things.

The next day we took Jaimie for a checkup. A blood test showed she was anemic, so the doctor sent us straight to the children's hospital. Little did we realize that this would be the first of hundreds of visits.

After more tests, the diagnosis was frightening: Jaimie had acute myeloid leukemia. The doctor told us that it's more common among adults and is very difficult to treat. As we studied this horrible disease, grim reality began to dawn.

When Jaimie began chemotherapy, our lives changed dramatically. Although Robert was very busy with ministry, we took turns staying at the hospital overnight. It was well worth the sleepless nights to know that we were with our Jaimie.

A month after starting chemotherapy, Jaimie called, saying, "Mum, my hair is coming out. I can pull it right off." I muffled my sobs as I thought of her long, black, curly hair.

It was so hard to see Jaimie's great pain and to helplessly hold her as she vomited. In desperation I longed for God to tell me why she had to suffer so. Somehow He gave just what we needed to get through each day.

Six months after her diagnosis, Jaimie went into remission and was allowed to come home. We were so excited! Although she had to go to the hospital once a week for blood tests, our lives seemed to be getting back to normal.

Three months into remission we went for another routine visit. The results were not good. Jaimie was unexpectedly having a relapse. We met with the doctors to find out what to do next. They told us that since her remission had not lasted long enough, another round of chemotherapy wouldn't help. They advised us to let nature take its course. There was nothing else for them to do.

When I came out of the doctor's office, I collapsed against the wall in the waiting room and wept. Although I was aware of people around me, I couldn't hide the pain of thinking about losing Jaimie. With tears streaming, I prayed and cried out to the Lord. And He answered. Miraculously, God's perfect peace flooded over me somehow and seemed to drown my sorrows. But God wasn't finished. That night He gave two vivid dreams to me that brought great comfort.

The next day God gave me Isa. 26:3. "You will keep in perfect peace him whose mind is steadfast, because he trusts in you." I claimed it, because God always delivers His promises.

We prayed for a miracle. As we sadly watched Jaimie's health deteriorate, we thanked God for each day. We were constantly amazed at the ways Jaimie found to comfort us since she realized she would be leaving us soon. During her final days with us she spoke freely about death and heaven.

One day as our family was driving by a cemetery, Jaimie asked, "Mum, am I going to be in one of those when I die?"

Trying to hide my pain, I explained, "If you die, your body will be there, but your spirit will live with the Lord in heaven forever." Since she had accepted the Lord as her Savior when she was four, we wanted to assure her that when she left us she would be in heaven.

When we were feeling sad, our seven-year-old Jamie encouraged us by saying, "We must trust the Lord." Her faith never wavered. Her courage was a living testimony to the very end.

During the last weeks of her life, Jaimie spoke on the radio about her sickness and shared her faith in Christ. The radio station staff and many listeners were deeply touched by her maturity and commitment to the Lord. Some gave their hearts to the Lord because of Jaimie's testimony.

Jaimie passed away at home the morning of September 26, 1988. As I held her in my arms and watched her take her last breath, God miraculously sustained me with His perfect peace.

God taught many lessons to me through our tragic loss. Now I listen to others who are going through testing times, and I pray faithfully for them. I tell them about God's peace.

For in the midst of deepest tragedy and loss, God gave me peace that passes human understanding. And that's the greatest lesson I can share.

Prayer: *Thank you, Father, for your perfect peace.*

Thought for the Day: Although God may not take us *out of* trying times, He'll take us *through* them.

41  THE DAY WE CROSSED KELLOGG

joyce williams

*You will be my witnesses in Jerusalem, and in all
Judea and Samaria, and to the ends of the earth.*
—Acts 1:8

The warm spring breeze caressed our faces that Saturday morning as we walked the streets of our church's neighborhood just across Kellogg (called the "Yellow Brick Road"). These six lanes of zooming traffic slice across Wichita, Kansas, severing us from our "Jerusalem."

In my quiet times with the Lord, He had profoundly laid a burden on my heart for our church neighborhood. Finally, several of us agreed to call on our neglected neighbors in that transient, inner-city area. Drive-by shootings are not uncommon there, and drugs have become a way of life for many. This little pocket is filled with people who need to know that Jesus loves them and so do we. We had prayed that the Holy Spirit would go before us, open hearts, and protect us. Then we got into our cars, drove under the overpass, parked, and began knocking on doors, careful to keep each other in sight.

My first door was opened hesitantly by a curly-haired little boy named Trevor. He yelled, "Mama! Somebody's here!" Somewhat reluctantly, his mother, Sharon, came to the door. I introduced myself and asked if she attended church.

She said, "Yeah, sometimes." However, she was uncertain of her church's name (a big clue!).

So I pointed over my left shoulder and said, "My husband pastors that church across Kellogg. We'd sure love for you and Trevor to come to visit with us."

About that time, two 12-year-old boys rode up on their bikes. Sharon introduced me to her son, Kenny, and his friend, Stephen. I asked them if they went to church. Very emphatically they replied in unison with a resounding "No!"

Again I pointed over my shoulder to my church. Stephen said, "My mama and I—we don't do church."

I said, "But, guys, we have a great gym where kids play ball." Suddenly their eyes lit up with a spark of interest as I told them about teen activities.

Then Stephen said, "Like I said, my mom and I really don't like church stuff. But I have a little brother named David who really does."

Intrigued, I said, "I'd sure like to meet David."

Stephen said, "Follow me!"

Sharon promised to visit Sunday. Then Larry, our children's pastor, joined me.

Stephen leaned his bike against the tumbledown front porch and yelled into the house, "David! Somebody wants to talk to you." Almost immediately a tow-headed eight-year-old erupted from the front door.

I told him who I was and pointed up the street to the church. Then I said, "David, Stephen tells me you like God and going to church."

Without hesitation he immediately responded, "I sure do. Some nights I even get Mom to pray with me before I go to sleep."

Several people wandered in and out of the house as we talked. Then I asked David, "Do you have friends who don't go to church?"

He replied, "Yep—bunches. And they sure *need* church." When I asked if he would like to introduce me to his neighbors, he quickly responded, "You betcha!" He said his stepdad was at home, so I said, "Let's make sure it's OK for you to go."

When Larry and I stepped into the living room, David introduced us to Jim, his stepfather. Several men were in the house with Jim, and I noticed they were acting a little strange. After getting Jim's permission, we quickly returned to the front porch with David.

As we started down the steps, a car pulled into the driveway. A thin, pretty blonde in tight shorts and tee-shirt opened the door, her cigarette dangling. David said, "Hi, Mom!" She waved, flipped her cigarette away, and began to unload groceries. I walked over to her and introduced myself. She said, "My name's Vicki."

Then David said, "Dad said I could go with them to talk about their church. OK?"

She shrugged her shoulders and said, "I guess so. Be careful now. You hear?"

As she turned to open the door, I stepped across a hole in the porch and asked, "Vicki, could I pray with you and David before we go?"

She said, "I reckon." I put my hands on their shoulders and prayed a brief prayer asking God to bless their home.

Imagine my amazement when I looked up and saw black rivers coursing down Vicki's cheeks! I'll never forget what she said as she wiped away her tears. "All my life my mama, who's a radio preacher from Newton, Kansas, has prayed that somebody like you would knock on my door. Mama kept praying and trusting all these years that we would get back to God." She brushed more tears away and promised to be in church the next day.

Just then Larry emerged from the house, and we set off with David leading the way, going from house to house. Finally David said, "Do you like old people?"

"Why sure," I replied. Then he led us to a home several blocks away where he mowed the grass. A man opened the door and invited us to come in even though he and his mother were eating lunch. David introduced us to Richard and Neila, and we talked with them while their soup cooled.

When Neila answered the phone, Richard began to share about his fears. There was a heart hunger in his eyes. I presented the gospel to Richard and then asked if he would like to have the peace and joy in his life that come only through knowing Christ. He quickly answered, "Yes!" By then Neila returned, and we all joined hands. With David right in the middle, they accepted the Lord as their Savior. I was reminded of the scripture "A little child will lead them" (Isa. 11:6).

Larry and I walked David backed home and rejoined the others. We could hardly wait for Sunday to see how many would really come. Imagine our delight when 18 came including Sharon, Trevor, Kenny, Vicki, Stephen, David, Richard, and Neila! About 14 new people came to Monday night open gym. But there were many struggles ahead.

We soon discovered that Jim and Vicki were addicted to drugs. They told me later that we had interrupted a drug deal that Saturday at their house. No wonder so many people were traipsing in and out! Jim later told me that when I said, "Hi!" he should have responded, "Yes, I am!"

The next week David's family was evicted from their house. Our Affirmers Class helped them find another place to live, but they soon dropped out of sight. Sharon, Trevor, and Richard became very faithful and regular attenders. David came sporadically. A few months later Sharon joined the church.

About 18 months later, I had finished teaching our Affirmers Class on Sunday morning when an usher rushed to get me. He said, "The Rolands are here." Incredulously, I hurried up the stairs. I could hardly believe my eyes. There stood Vicki Roland—looking great! In my own "tactful" way I said, "Vicki, what happened to you? You're stunning!" She quickly replied, smiling from ear to ear, "I gave my heart to God and quit drugs!"

Tears streamed down my face as I hugged her, and we did a little dance of joy right there in the church foyer. Then she said, "Jimmy's here, and he wants to see you."

I followed her into the sanctuary, and there sat that long-haired, toothless addict. I sat down beside him and told him I had never stopped praying for them. He said, "It's worked, because I've come today to give my heart to God!"

I said, "Great! Come sit with me." And they followed me down the aisle. (They didn't know about not sitting on the front rows!)

As soon as the invitation was given at the close of the service, Jim nudged me and said, "Excuse me." He stepped into the aisle and knelt at the altar. Jim quit drugs "cold turkey" right then.

There have been many tough times for Jim and Vicki, but they brought many people to church with them. One of the most touching moments was when Jim portrayed a thief on the cross in our "Living Pictures of Easter" drama—two years in a row. Oh, yes—Jim was the thief who went to paradise!

A few Sundays after Jim and Vicki were saved, our hearts were deeply moved when they and Richard joined the church. That Sunday evening the entire congregation applauded when they were baptized. Jim and Vicki conducted a backyard Bible School the following summer with more than 50 kids attending. Several gave their hearts to the Lord. Jim and Sharon helped with After School Adventure, a latchkey program for a neighborhood school. Richard remained after class each Sunday to clean the coffeepot.

A few months later Stephen asked Jim, "Am I old enough to go to that class and join the church?" When Jim asked me, I said an enthusiastic "Yes!" He and his mom had come a long way from that day when he told me they didn't "do church!"

When God led Gene to resign as pastor a few years later, it was quite hard on these "lambs." But recently we were back at the church, and what a blessing to see Sharon and Trevor still faithfully attending each Sunday! Richard was still making coffee for the Affirmers Class.

We stay in close touch with Jim and Vicki. As a matter of fact, when Vicki's sweet preacher mother died, Gene conducted her funeral. Filling that void, Vicki has emerged as the spiritual matriarch of her family. They serve as prayer partners for us and support our ministry.

All I can say is—I'm so glad we crossed the street that day!

Prayer: *Father, give us courage to be your witnesses, beginning in our Jerusalem.*

Thought for the Day: Many times God's divine appointments are just across the street.

42 GOD'S FORMULA

frances simpson

*"You shall love the LORD your God with all your heart,
with all your soul, and with all your mind." This is the
first and great commandment. And the second is like it:
"You shall love your neighbor as yourself."*
—Matt. 22:37-39, NKJV

I finished preparing dinner, trying to appear calm. Instead of setting our green dinette table in our tiny kitchen for the three of us, I set two places—one for my husband, Eugene, and one for Mark, our 18-month-old son. I quickly wiped away a tear as I heard the door opening. Mark and I met Eugene at the door, and then we went to the kitchen.

Before Eugene could ask, "Why two places instead of three?" I explained that I was fasting and was going to our bedroom to pray as soon as he and Mark were served. "I'm not coming out until God helps me!" I declared.

Now that's quite a bold statement. But I was tired of feeling downcast and out-of-sync in this, our second church assignment. The problem was not that I didn't want to be a pastor's wife. When I married my husband, I knew that his call would become my call and that it would define my life in many ways. I just wasn't doing a good job.

Our first church had been an exciting one. And, yes, I had fit in all right. The church grew, we built a new sanctuary, and I felt pretty-much at home. Then the district superintendent asked us to take another home mission church that had been planted just nine months earlier. We had a small building with about 40 wonderful people in a beautiful oceanside town. I should have been happy, but I wasn't.

I still remember going to our bedroom that evening, closing the door, and falling prostrate across our bed. Eventually I moved to the floor as I fought my internal battle with self. I now knew it all boiled down to an identity problem. I was still in my 20s and had no relatives nearby. The church was my family. But we didn't know each other yet. Furthermore, I was convinced they liked the founding pastor's wife better than they liked me.

I presented my case before the Lord. *Father, why do I feel this way? I believe you saved me when I was 11 years old. To the best of my ability I committed my life to you then. So why am I struggling?*

Satan popped up. *Why, you just aren't cut out to be a pastor's wife. Your parents weren't brought up in church. You can't play the piano. You're afraid to talk in front of people.*

I continued to lay out my case. *Lord, did you really save me back then, or was I too young to make that kind of decision?*

As God always does, He began to talk back to me: *Have you taken anything off the altar?*

No, Lord, I cried. *To the best of my knowledge, everything is still there.*

Then I tried to change the subject. *Lord, these people don't care a thing about my past. They don't care that I was an honor student. They don't care that I was football queen. They don't care where I've been or what I've done.*

It was then that the Lord jolted me with a simple question: *Do you know what these people want from you? They want you to love me with all your heart. Then they want you to love them and show it.* God had given His formula to me.

I think I can do that, Lord, I answered.

Later that night when I told Eugene about my encounter with God, he said, "I'm so glad! I was thinking I might have to leave the pastorate to make you happy!"

That was more than 45 years ago. I still thank God for personalizing Matt. 22:37-39 for me and then helping me live it out these many years. Loving God and others works itself out in all kinds of ways and has helped me do things I never dreamed I could.

The way of love—God's formula—is a recipe for joy that endures forever.

Prayer: *Father, thank you for programming your love into me and then teaching me to share it with those around me. Hug someone through me today.*

Thought for the Day: God's love stretches us into conformity to His will for our lives.

43 HURRICANES, EAGLES, AND BABY PRAYERS

mary tabb

In the shadow of your wing, I find protection
until the raging storms are over.
—Ps. 57:1, TEV

Hurricanes happen! At least they do in my world of southern Louisiana.

The day before I was to leave our daughter's home in Denver, we began watching The Weather Channel as a huge tropical storm headed toward the Gulf Coast. When I called the airlines, I was told that all flights had been canceled.

The next morning, August 29, 2005, Hurricane Katrina smashed into the Gulf Coast, leaving a path of destruction that would be felt by millions. Glued to the television set, I could scarcely believe my eyes: towns were leveled and cities were flooded, forcing thousands to flee their homes. Then in New Orleans the levees were breached, followed by unprecedented flooding and human suffering. Thousands were evacuated. It was like living in *The Twilight Zone.*

During the first weeks after the hurricane hit, we continued to see and hear the urgent cries for help from thousands needing water, food, shelter—the basics for survival. Relief came from churches, private agencies, the government, and from individuals wanting to help.

But there was another group, mostly children and young people, who had been calling for help, praying to God for help, for a long time before Katrina. They had been trapped in a life of suffering, corruption, and misery with little hope of getting out. Many had barely survived the horrors of pain, deprivation, and sorrow. Their culture was rife with drugs, crime, and prostitution. Who could deliver them? How could they ever be free of danger? Where could they find a safe place?

The answers can be found in the Scriptures. Psalm 91:1-2 says, "Those who live in the shelter of the Most High will find rest in the shadow of the Almighty. This I declare of the LORD: he alone is my refuge, my place of safety; he is my God and I am trusting him" (NLT). Were any of these children living in the shelter of the Most High? Were any of them calling out to the almighty God of the universe? Were any trusting Him? I was soon to discover the answer to these questions also.

For nine years my friends Hy and Libba McEnery have worked as missionaries with Child Evangelism in New Orleans' inner city. They've had the joy of seeing more than 3,000 children put their faith in Christ for salvation. They taught many of them how to read and memorize scripture, pray, and tell others about Jesus.

The McEnerys believe that one of the good things to

come as a result of Katrina is that many of these children have finally been rescued from their lives of untold suffering. Their calls and "baby prayers" have been heard and answered by their loving Heavenly Father. They surely have the faith to remove mountains!

One of these children is Herbert, now 18. For nine years Herbert was faithfully taught the Word of God. He was taught that when God said something in His Word and he believed it in his heart, that settled it. Because he had received a limited education, Herbert's reading skills tested lower than average. For this reason, he could relate more easily to word pictures in the Scriptures, quickly grasping concepts like "rock," "fortress," "sun," "shield," and "eagle." He so wanted to rise above his difficulties and hardships that he was especially drawn to the description of mounting up with wings of eagles found in Isa. 40:31.

When he was 14 he started a little church in the small kitchen of his house. He preached, and his five sisters sang. Nearly 30 people crammed into the room. The most important part of the meetings was the prayer time. The children prayed to be rescued from the alcohol and drug culture. They cried out to God for loved ones who were lost and in prison. They prayed for America, New Orleans, for the corrupt politicians in city government. They prayed for deliverance from their schools, where they were not effectively taught how to read. No doubt these "baby prayers" went straight to the throne of grace.

When Katrina hit, Herbert, his mother, and his five sisters

lived in the lower Ninth Ward of New Orleans, a short distance from where the levees broke. They watched as their house floated away and were soon evacuated to the Superdome.

The week they were there they witnessed it all: dead bodies, suicide, rape, knifings, shootings, looting, and continuous cries for rescue. So Herbert prayed. Herbert asked God to help him know what to do to help these poor souls. He woke up knowing what to do. He started to march around the dome singing gospel songs and choruses. Little by little, people joined him, and before long there was a second line doing the same thing. Then people began to pray audibly, calling out to God for help. Herbert knew then that this is what God had led him to do. He talked to people in small, impromptu Bible studies. Within one day there were 50 groups meeting informally both in the morning and in the evening before curfew.

From these meetings, people caught a spark of hope and words of encouragement. Herbert's message was simple: "Trust the Lord. He has not deserted us." He knew that God's Word said, "God is our refuge and strength, A very present help in trouble. Therefore we will not fear" (Ps. 46:1-2, NKJV).

Finally, Herbert and his family were relocated to Lake Charles, Louisiana. Within a day or two, he was accepted into a Christian school where he could not only finish his high school education but also play football. Within two weeks, however, Hurricane Rita hit. Tragically, they were forced to evacuate again, this time to the River Center Shelter in Baton Rouge. Though it wasn't as bad as the Superdome, it was still a far cry from the answer to his prayers.

Was God watching? Yes, the "eagle eye" of God was alert, watching everything and doing some marvelous things for Herbert. Far away in a little town in Iowa, a small missionary-minded church devised a plan to rescue some of the evacuees. They sent their copastor with an air-conditioned bus to Louisiana to meet with the McEnerys to try to get Herbert, his family, and some others who had been in his little church to evacuate to Iowa. It didn't take much persuasion before 18 people were loaded onto the bus with tears of thanksgiving streaming down their faces.

When they arrived in Iowa, they found that the church had procured houses for them, food had been stocked on the shelves, and beds had been made with individual nametags on each. And when they finally drifted into an exhausted sleep that first night in Iowa, Herbert and some of his congregation's dreams "soared like eagles" climbing into the sky.

Today all school-aged children are in school, and those who can work have found jobs. Herbert, the young "Moses," and those of his flock have completed their exodus. Their "baby prayers" have been answered.

Prayer: *Father, as strange as it may sound, I thank you for the storms.*

Thought for the Day: May our baby prayers soar on eagle's wings above the storms of life.

LOVING HER NEIGHBOR

joyce williams

Love your neighbor as yourself.
—Matt. 19:19

I became a pastor's wife in the "middle ages" of my life. To be perfectly honest, I was somewhat intimidated by the challenges. My husband's first wife, Bettye, had been the ultimate wife, mother, and ministry mate. There was no way I could fill her shoes. But I earnestly wanted to be God's best person in my new role.

One of the first things I did after we were married was to prayerfully seek out mentors and models who were veterans of many years of ministry. I was tremendously blessed to have a virtual smorgasbord of kind ladies nearby. I eagerly sought their counsel and wisdom.

One of my favorites was Evalena Jones. She and her dear husband, Harold, served together in full-time ministry for more than 40 years. One of the neatest things about them was observing how their "pastoring" had not ended with retirement from ministering to a local congregation. However, I must state right off that "retirement" is not a term that ever really fit them. Although they may not have had their own parish, they continued to work hard and to fill many pulpits.

One of the ways I was most blessed by their example is how they literally took to heart the Master's instruction to love their neighbor.

Pastor Harold and Evalena lived in a rather modest home in a quiet neighborhood. When a lady named Elizabeth, who was from Colombia, married their next-door neighbor, an immediate bond formed with the Joneses. Elizabeth shared how she had come to know Jesus as a child through a missionary in Colombia who was from Kansas. It wasn't long before Elizabeth began attending Sunday school and church with Harold and Evalena.

Elizabeth was very close to her family in Colombia, and she was homesick for them. In those months it was truly divinely ordered that Evalena became her second mother. When her mother came to visit, Elizabeth introduced Evalena as her "number-two mother".

When Elizabeth's two children were born, Harold and Evalena immediately became "Grandpa and Grandma." A very special love flowed between these two families.

Later as Elizabeth began to have marriage problems, Harold and Evalena became a safe haven for her and the children as divorce loomed on the horizon. They prayed with her and shared scripture as they encouraged Elizabeth to hold steady in her Christian faith. The church family wrapped their arms around this wonderful little family as well.

After the divorce was finalized, Harold and Evalena fully stepped into the void and helped this courageous single mother. Although Elizabeth and the children moved several miles away, they stayed very close, continuing to be neighbors and family at heart.

When Harold passed away at the age of 91, Elizabeth and her children grieved deeply for "Grandpa." They continue to keep in daily contact with "Grandma." Their calls and visits help to fill the lonely void in Evalena's days.

Elizabeth says that Evalena has been an "angel" to her. "Her love never stops—it's so special. I always knew that she and Grandpa loved us and would be there for us anytime we needed them. And Grandma still is there for us today."

Evalena continues to demonstrate in very tangible ways the essence of what it means to remain a constant and genuine neighbor. She keeps her door and heart open to be there for those who need an encouraging word. As Elizabeth says, "Grandma's love is *so big!*"

I thank God for a marvelous mentor and model who has established a pattern throughout her life of loving her neighbors. She has totally embraced our Lord's command as she continues to lovingly share her heart and life.

I must add that I'm especially grateful that God also moved me into Evalena's "neighborhood."

Prayer: *Father, please help us to care genuinely about those around us. May we always be sensitive to their needs as we reach out, while keeping our love "big."*

Thought for the Day: "Above all, love each other deeply" (1 Pet. 4:8).

45 GOD IS SPEAKING. ARE YOU LISTENING?

melody tunney

He makes me lie down in green pastures. . . . He restores my soul.
—Ps. 23:2-3

You may have read Ps. 23 hundreds of times, as I have, and not noticed one little word in particular. He *makes* me lie down. Have you ever been *made* to lie down? Several years ago the Lord allowed two different incidents in my life that caused me to learn to listen.

I've been in music ministry for more than 25 years and have been blessed with many wonderful opportunities to serve the Lord. Whether in the recording studio, performing in groups like TRUTH and First Call, or ministering with my husband, Dick, in local churches, God has opened many doors where I've been blessed to use my voice for His service.

In the fall of 2000, I began to have some difficulty singing and was diagnosed with a polyp on my right vocal chord. For a singer, this is not good news. This particular type of polyp,

I was told, could be removed surgically only. My doctors strongly suggested I schedule surgery. With the recovery time, there would be three to four months of relearning how to speak and sing. At the time, Dick and I had dates on the calendar with approximately 45 weekends a year already scheduled. There was no window of time to take this kind of break. We enlisted family and friends to pray for two things. Obviously, we prayed that God would heal me. Second, we prayed that if His way of healing me was to be surgical, He would give us the wisdom to know which four months of concert dates to cancel.

During the next few months, my routine was to be quiet during the week and save my voice for singing on the weekends. It was a frustrating time, trying to be quiet and lead a normal life as wife and the mother of two teenage girls.

Several months passed. The prayers continued. I felt my voice getting stronger, and yet every two weeks when I went to my vocal doctor for a check-up, his response would be the same: "The polyp isn't getting any smaller. You need to schedule the surgery."

On January 4, 2001, as I was dressing to go to another doctor's appointment, I prayed, *Lord, make me content with whatever happens today. If the polyp is still the same, please give me wisdom about what to do.*

I immediately heard that still, small voice say to me, "Expect the unexpected."

I responded, *Lord, did you really say that? Am I to expect something unexpected today?* Immediately Eph. 3:20 came to mind: "[God] is able to do immeasurably more than all we ask or imagine, according to his power that is at work within us."

When I got to the doctor's office, he placed the scope down my throat as he always did. But when he saw my vocal chords, he simply stopped and said, "Hmm."

My husband, who was there with me, said, "Hmm—what?"

The doctor replied, "I think you've had a Christmas miracle. The polyp is completely gone." Needless to say, next came many tears, phone calls, and much celebration. God had healed me!

The story doesn't end there. Six months later, our family was preparing to be at a family camp where Chuck Swindoll would speak and Dick and I would be leading worship. The day before we were to leave, I began having vision problems. Within 12 hours I had gone completely blind in my right eye. The doctor diagnosed a detached retina and scheduled immediate surgery.

The recovery required lying down on my right side 24 hours a day for several weeks. I could get up only to go to the bathroom or eat, but other than that, no reading, no television, nothing that caused eye movement. It was during this period that God began to speak loudly, and I learned what it meant to listen. The "green pastures" I was *made* to lie down in was my own home.

I learned valuable lessons through these two events. God is not as interested in my ability as in my *avail*ability to Him. He's always speaking. But are we listening?

Prayer: *Father, thank you for the trials you bring my way that draw me closer to you. Help me embrace life's difficulties—always listening for your voice.*

Thought for the Day: What is God saying today?

46 UNEXPECTED WAVES, UNEXPECTED BLESSINGS

sharon joy underwood

Fear not, for I am with you; Be not be dismayed,
for I am your God. I will strengthen you, Yes, I will help you.
—Isa. 41:10, NKJV

I remember the sun coming up as on any other day that spring morning in 2004. My husband, Teddy, was slowly navigating the boat of our older son, Jamey, through the inlet at Fort Pierce, Florida. The Florida humidity, the smell of the salt water, and the occasional fish jumping were all par for the course. As we began to gain speed, Suzanna, Jamey's fiancé (now wife) and I headed to the bow of the boat and sat facing each other.

Three big waves came at us in quick succession. We laughed about the first one. I tightened my grip for the second. I never saw the other side of wave number three, because it threw me to the floor of the boat.

Everything around me went black. Something was very wrong with my back. The doctor later told us that it was caused by a combination of things—my sitting posture, the speed of the boat, and the angle of my spine. I could hear screams but couldn't distinguish voices. Jamey was telling me that everything was going to be all right, but I could barely understand him through my crying. He kept saying, "I've got you, Mom. It's OK." My mind raced to the only logical conclusion: the screams were mine. Then the pain kicked in, but it was short-lived as I went into numbing shock. The boat was turned around, and we headed for shore.

We tend to think of God as having our steps laid out for the good, but God leads our steps on the other side of the bad as well. And He was about to make this quite clear to me.

Although we hadn't radioed for help, an ambulance was awaiting our arrival—the crew had stopped by the beach for lunch. In a few moments I was strapped onto a backboard and whisked away to the hospital.

Under the squeal of the siren, fading in and out of consciousness, I heard the driver say to the dispatcher, "possible spinal injury." *Please, God,* I prayed as I faded back into the blackness, *let me walk again.* The church we pastor was really taking off. Teddy needed me.

The emergency room was full, and I appeared to be last on the list. Finally, they took X-rays. I began thanking God for the healing that would take place regardless of what was wrong.

After three hours, the doctor came in. She stood over me saying, "Mrs. Underwood, you have a broken back." With a squinty-eyed prayer, I shot back under my breath, "In the name of Jesus, no, I don't!" She told me she needed to see a few more people before finishing up with me, but God had a better plan.

Just as the doctor was turning away, Teddy rounded the corner. When he said, "Tina?" her face lit up.

"Hi, Teddy", she replied. "Why are you here?"

Then, looking back at me, she made the connection. Her voice changed from that of a fast-paced doctor to that of a loving caregiver. She looked at Teddy once more. "Let me see what I can do to speed this along." Teddy looked down at me and smiled, saying, "Tina's our new neighbor."

Five minutes later Tina returned with a special blessing. She had bumped into my family doctor in the hall. Although my faith was strong, God knew I was afraid. So He had arranged that meeting of doctors. I got the feeling that He wanted me to be assured that He knew where I was and was taking care of me.

An MRI revealed a compressed fracture and a burst fracture of my spine. Though I would need to wear a back brace for the next six months, the specialist believed I would heal fine on my own and would not need surgery. I remembered Isa. 41:10.

Three months later I was told I no longer needed the back brace. My six-month check-up revealed a faster overall healing track than the doctors had anticipated. The specialist referred to me as a miracle. I told him, "It's all because of God, and of course my good doctor."

He smiled and said, "I don't think I had anything to do with this one."

Prayer: *Father, help me to realize that no matter what comes my way, I'm your child, and you'll take care of me.*

Thought for the Day: An unexpected blessing is waiting for us every day. We just have to believe.

47

PARTNERING WITH ANGEL

joyce williams

He will command His angels concerning you to
guard you in all your ways.
—Ps. 91:11

The flickering lights captured the radiant faces glowing in the darkness our last night in India. Srinivas, the little pastor, led the music, his hands pounding his drum with perfect rhythm as the sound swelled throughout the little village. People kept crowding into the tiny room, cramming in from wall to wall with others standing outside. The pastor's wife, Savitha, ran to get a lantern as the lights dimmed once again. She didn't have far to go. Their little parsonage was just a doorway away from the tiny sanctuary.

For almost two weeks my husband, Gene, and I had enjoyed being with our friends Pastor Solomon and Selvi Mary Dinakaran. Their family has become very dear to us, and we especially enjoyed being with their three wonderful children. Once again, we had spoken in many places and shared unforgettable experiences.

As Gene spoke, I looked out over that dear group and was reminded, *This is why we keep coming to India—these precious people.* Tears filled my eyes as I realized that we had only a few more hours before we would say goodbye.

After the service we met the people clasping hands and sharing their hearts. Then Pastor Srinivas came to me and said, "Aunty, I want you to meet someone." He led me to Padma, a young mother, and her three-year-old twin daughters named Martha and Mariya. As I looked into her careworn face and grasped her calloused hands, he said, "She's working at menial tasks cleaning toilets, sweeping the streets—anything she can do to try to scrape together enough money so they can survive. Her husband abandoned them, and she has no one to help her." My tears flowed as I looked into the precious faces of those two little girls.

Then Pastor Srinivas said, "Could I show you where they live?" I followed him across the narrow, rutted, dusty village to their tiny hovel. Stepping over a sleeping dog, I walked into that windowless room no larger than my bedroom closet. In a tiny corner I saw the blackened wall and charcoal grill. That was their kitchen. Only a few worn garments hung on nails on the wall. Pastor Srinivas said, "At night Padma can't stretch her legs out fully when they sleep. I'm very concerned about this little family."

I knew we had to help them—to make sure they would be OK. But how could I do that from the other side of the world? I tenderly hugged those beautiful girls and their mother one more time. As we bounced along the rutted road back to our hotel, my heart ached as my mind raced. What *could* I do? I could hardly get to sleep for thinking of their pitiful plight. I prayed, *Lord, please show me what to do.* Finally I drifted off to sleep.

When I awoke about three o'clock the next morning, my thoughts immediately flashed to that little family as I pictured them huddling together on thin mats on that dusty floor. Once again I prayed tearfully in the dark. We could leave some money, but they needed more than that. The girls needed someone to spend time with them and care for them.

And then the answer came. The Dinakarans' younger daughter was in college studying to be a social worker—a "Mother Teresa" to those in great need. Their home was just a few kilometers away. She could be my partner in caring for that little family!

As we gathered the next morning to make a final shopping run into the old city, Selvi Mary, her girls, and others were so excited. There was a sale at the Half Price Sari Shop! Over the constant cacophony of blaring horns, I shared my concerns as our driver wove through a river of vehicles of every description. Then I turned to Selvi Mary's younger daughter and asked, "Could you adopt this little family as a special project? Would you be able to visit them and care for them?"

Her eyes glowed as she said, "Oh, yes, Aunty! I would love to spend time with them and make sure they're all right." Her smile stretched from ear to ear.

Then it dawned on me: God had more than answered my prayers. He had provided just what He has promised to do always—send His special emissaries to care for our needs. My heart swelled with joy! You see, the name of my beautiful young partner and collaborator who would carry on with this dear mother and her precious twins is *Angel*!

Prayer: *Father, may we always be aware of divine appointments with your angels.*

Thought for the Day: What a blessing to realize that our Father allows us to participate in His miracles!

48

QUIET MOMENTS

joyce williams

Father, in Your Word we read
  That Your Son often withdrew
To solitary places
  To spend time alone with You.

Those precious, intimate times
  Cherished by Father and Son
Are models we must follow
  So life's battles may be won.

But I confess sometimes it's hard
  To truly be still and wait
When pressures of daily life
  Seem overwhelmingly great.

But those times are when I most
  Need to step out of the race
As I pause to listen for
  Your words of love, hope, and grace.

For it's in those quiet moments
  Carved from life's frantic pace
That I hear your sweet, gentle whisper
  That soothes my turbulent days.

So today I seek Your heart
  In this quiet and sheltered place
To wait and listen for You
  To calm my day's hectic pace.

Then when storms rage all around
  And floods threaten to break through,
I know that You'll be with me
  'Cause I've spent time alone with You.

ABOUT THE CONTRIBUTORS

Jeannie McCullough: Jeannie founded Wisdom of the Word (WOW) Bible Study in 1986 when she and her husband, Mel, were pastoring in Bethany, Oklahoma. WOW has now expanded to Children of the Word, prison ministries, and missions around the world. They live in Olathe, Kansas.

Gladys Staines: Gladys and her late husband, Graham, served as missionaries to leprosy sufferers in India for many years. Graham had worked in India for 18 years prior to their marriage in 1983, and Graham and Gladys continued their work there until his death. She and her daughter, Esther, live in Queensland, Australia.

Joyce Baggott: Joyce was a pastor's wife for more than 26 years. She taught school for several years and later directed a learning center. Joyce is a cancer survivor who works alongside her husband, Barney, who is the district superintendent of the North Arkansas District of the Church of the Nazarene. They have three children and several grandchildren. They live in Fort Smith, Arkansas.

Sheila Bird: Sheila recently completed two master's degrees in business. In addition to working full time, she ministers alongside her husband, Don, who pastors in Overland Park, Kansas. They have four children.

Cindy Blasdel: Cindy works alongside her husband, Steve, who is minister of worship at their church. They have ministered together nearly 27 years. She teaches music classes at Friends University. Cindy and Steve have three children and twin grandchildren. They live in Wichita, Kansas.

Sally Bond: Sally has enjoyed partnering with her husband, Jim, in the pastorate and as missionaries. Jim has been a university president as well as general superintendent in the Church of the Nazarene. They have two children and seven grandchildren. They live in Colorado Springs.

Vonette Bright: Vonette and her late husband, Bill, cofounded Campus Crusade for Christ in 1951. She is an accomplished author and speaker. She is the founder of the National Prayer Committee and serves as chairwoman of the National Day of Prayer Task Force. Vonette was instrumental in establishing the National Day of Prayer. In 1993 she launched Women Today International. She lives in Orlando, Florida.

Jennifer Buettner: Jennifer has served alongside her pastor-husband, Harlan, for more than 26 years. She is an accomplished musician and enjoys playing the piano. The Buettners have one son and live in Seattle.

Myrna Buhler: Myrna has been a pastor's wife and partner in ministry with her husband, Brian, for 26 years. They have one daughter and live in North Vancouver, British Columbia.

Rachael Crabb: Rachael speaks at retreats and conferences worldwide. She serves on the national board of Stonecroft Ministries and as a Denver area prayer consultant. She leads two Bible studies each week. She is a published author and serves on the advisory board for MOPS (Mothers of Preschoolers). She and her husband have two sons and grandchildren. They live in Morrison, Colorado.

Betty Daily: Betty and her husband, Bob, pastored for more than 35 years. In addition to participating in many mission trips, Betty has been active in local and district missions and women's ministries. She and Bob have three grown sons and live in Nashville.

Susan Dillow: Susan served beside her husband, Jim, in pastoral ministry for 31 years. Jim now serves in Missouri as district superintendent for the Church of the Nazarene, and Susan does substitute teaching. They have two grown sons. They live in Carthage, Missouri.

Denise Franklin: Denise has served in ministry with her husband, Kendall, for nearly 25 years as he has pastored in California, Oklahoma, and Kansas. They have three sons. They live in Hutchinson, Kansas.

Kendra Graham: Kendra is a registered nurse. She works at a hospital and serves with her husband, Wil, who pastors in Wake Forest, North Carolina. Wil is following in the heritage of his grandfather Billy and father, Franklin, in evangelism and speaking at crusades. They have three children. They live in Wake Forest.

Karan Gunter: Karan is an elementary school teacher in Franklin, Tennessee. She teaches Sunday School, Bible studies, and serves as partner in ministry with her husband, Dwight, at Trevecca Community Church in Nashville.

Patty Hambrick: Patty and her husband, Ted, pastor New Direction Church in Beaufort, South Carolina. She is a college professor, conference speaker, and director of women's ministries in South Carolina. They live in Charleston, South Carolina.

Debbie Henry: Debbie has served alongside her husband, John, in ministry for more than 25 years. She is presently on staff at their church as coordinator for local missions and benevolence. They have three children. They live in Wichita, Kansas.

Mary Alice Hoover: Mary Alice serves with her husband, Mark, as he pastors Messiah Baptist Church in Wichita, Kansas. She is a Bible study teacher and administrator. They have three sons.

Joyce Jothi: Joyce grew up in the parsonage of the church her father pastored. She has completed her studies at Union Biblical Seminary in Pune, India, and works with her husband, Simon, who is a pastor and dean and registrar for South Asia Bible College India. They have two sons.

Debbie Keener: Deb holds a master's degree in educational psychology. She has chosen to focus on her family and Grace Fellowship in Albany, New York, where her husband, Rex, is senior pastor. She enjoys speaking and ministering to women. She and Rex have two children. They live in Cohoes, New York.

Linda Lewis: Linda has served in ministry with her husband, Ernie, for more than 37 years. They presently serve in Clearwater, Florida, where Linda is minister of music. They have two children and three grandchildren.

Gail MacDonald: Gail is a speaker, author, counselor, mother, grandmother, and ministry wife. She has ministered with her husband, Gordon, for 44 years as they have served five congregations. The MacDonalds live in Belmont, New Hampshire, near their children and five grandchildren.

Edie MacPherson: Edie and her husband, Corey, are leading a new church plant in Stony Brook, New York. Besides being a pastor's wife and the mother of two young children, Edie is assistant professor of communications at Suffolk County Community College. They live in Stony Brook.

Ellen McWhirter: Ellen and her husband, Stuart, have three grown children and one grandchild. When she is not traveling with her husband in evangelism, she spends her time with her grandson and cares for her elderly mother. They live in Corydon, Indiana.

Joyce Mehl: Joyce is a speaker and author. She ministered with her late husband, Ron, for 37 years. She now oversees their foundation, Compassion Ministries, and the radio broadcast, *Heart of the Word*. She also serves as chaplain for a children's hospital in Portland, Oregon.

Annie Montgomery: Annie has a heart for ministering to families through teaching, singing, preaching, and counseling. She serves with her husband, Lincoln, who is pastor of Tabernacle Baptist Church Without Walls. Annie served in the municipal government for 30 years. She and Lincoln have two children and grandchildren. They live in Wichita, Kansas.

Pam Morgan: Pam Morgan and her husband, Larry, have served together in ministry for more than 33 years. They have two children and six grandchildren. She serves as the district women's ministry director. They live in Wichita, Kansas.

Kelly Pankratz: Kelly and her husband, Bob, have worked together in ministry throughout their marriage. Their present ministry is The Oasis Ranch and Retreat Center in Plevna, Kansas, a place of refuge and retreat where lives can be restored. They have two children. They live in Plevna.

Jodie Pinckard: Jodie has taught in public schools since 1975 and has served in ministry with her husband, Phil. They share the story of their late son, Mark, as they speak about organ and tissue donation to various groups. They enjoy their daughter, Heather, and her family. They are authors of the book *Now Caitlin Can*. They live in El Dorado, Arkansas.

Nancy Roberts: Nancy received her music degrees from the University of Louisville. She taught many years in public schools and wrote a children's musical. She and her husband, Roger, live in Brussels, where he pastors the International Baptist Church of Brussels. They have two grown children.

Cheryl Roland: Cheryl has directed and worked with district and national women's ministries programs on several districts. Her husband, David, is Nazarene district superintendent in Indiana. They live in Marion, Indiana.

Pam Runyan: Pam is currently serving as worship pastor at a church near Houston, where she serves with her husband, Doug, who is senior pastor. They served as missionaries on the Ivory Coast of West Africa for 10 years before moving to Texas. They have three children and grandchildren. They live in Humble, Texas.

Gayla Ryan: Gayla and her husband, Larry, were in pastoral ministry for 25 years. They now serve as founders and directors of King's Way Foundation, an international compassionate relief organization. They live in Yukon, Oklahoma.

Cindy Schmelzenbach: Cindy is a missionary serving with her husband, Harmon, in the South Pacific. He is the director for Nazarene Maritime Ministries. They live with their two children in Suva in the Fiji Islands.

Laisa Siakimotu: Lisa is married to Robert, who serves with OAC Ministries International. She works as a learning assistant and is director of women's ministries at their church.

Frances Simpson: Frances has been married to her minister husband, Eugene, for 53 years. They have two children and five grandchildren. After serving as Nazarene district superintendent for North Carolina, the Simpsons are involved in their local church. She enjoys freelance writing. They live in Charlotte, North Carolina.

Mary Tabb: Mary ministered as a pastor's wife for more than 30 years alongside her husband, Donald. She is a professor at Louisiana State University. Mary is an accomplished speaker and author. The Tabbs have five adult children. They live in Baton Rouge, Louisiana.

Melody Tunney: Melody currently serves as worship director at her church in Franklin, Tennessee. She is also involved in concert ministry with her husband, Dick. They have two daughters. They live in Brentwood, Tennessee.

Sharon Joy Underwood: Sharon Joy and her husband, Ted, began ministering together when they were 18 years old, beginning in youth work. Sharon Joy leads women's ministries and teaches Bible studies. The Underwoods have two sons. They currently pastor in Fort Pierce, Florida.

Rise Above the Stereotypes!

Inspiration and Encouragement from Ministry Wives Just Like You

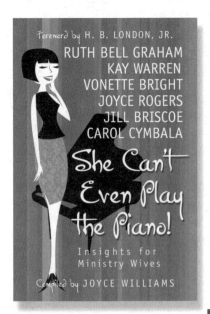

Foreword by H. B. LONDON, JR.

RUTH BELL GRAHAM
KAY WARREN
VONETTE BRIGHT
JOYCE ROGERS
JILL BRISCOE
CAROL CYMBALA

She Can't Even Play the Piano!

Insights for Ministry Wives

Compiled by JOYCE WILLIAMS

Featuring:

Ruth Bell Graham, Kay Warren,

Linda Armstrong, Oreta Burnham,

Beverly London, Linda Toler,

Joyce Rogers, Jill Briscoe,

Carol Cymbala, Vonetta Bright,

and others.

ISBN-13: 978-0-8341-2200-0

Full of stories from veteran ministry wives who have more than 1,000 years of combined experience, *She Can't Even Play the Piano!* provides insight and advice for balancing the demands of ministry and family while making time for one's own priorities as a pastor's wife.

She Can't Even Play the Piano! is guaranteed to encourage and uplift anyone who has ever felt overwhelmed by the stereotypical expectations that come when serving as a minister's wife.

BEACON HILL PRESS
OF KANSAS CITY

LOOK FOR IT WHEREVER CHRISTIAN BOOKS ARE SOLD.

More Life-Changing Stories of Faith...
...From Women Just Like You!

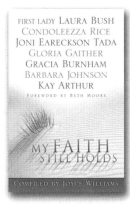

FIRST LADY LAURA BUSH
CONDOLEEZZA RICE
JONI EARECKSON TADA
GLORIA GAITHER
GRACIA BURNHAM
BARBARA JOHNSON
KAY ARTHUR

FOREWORD BY BETH MOORE

MY FAITH
STILL HOLDS

COMPILED BY JOYCE WILLIAMS

ISBN-13: 978-0-8341-2078-5

My Faith Still Holds
Featuring First Lady Laura Bush, Gracia Burnham, Barbara Johnson, and many others.

FOREWORD by BARBARA JOHNSON

UNSHAKABLE
FAITH for
SHAKY TIMES

LIZ CURTIS HIGGS • BETH MOORE
VONETTE BRIGHT • PATSY CLAIRMONT
PEGGY BENSON • and others
COMPILED by JOYCE WILLIAMS

ISBN-13: 978-0-8341-2020-4

Unshakable Faith for Shaky Times
Featuring Liz Curtis Higgs, Beth Moore, Vonette Bright, Peggy Benson, Patsy Clairmont, and others.

This book reminds us that all our trials—big ones
and little ones—matter to our Lord.
—Gary and Norma Smalley

ANNE GRAHAM LOTZ
GRACIA BURNHAM
LIZ CURTIS HIGGS
CHONDA PIERCE
BECKY TIRABASSI

FROM
THIS FAITH
FORWARD

COMPILED BY   FOREWORD BY
JOYCE WILLIAMS   JILL BRISCOE

ISBN-13: 978-0-8341-2186-7

From This Faith Forward
Featuring Anne Graham Lotz, Gracia Burnham, Becky Tirabassi, Chonda Pierce, and many others.

BEACON HILL PRESS
OF KANSAS CITY

Look for them wherever Christian books are sold!